THE ULTIMATE BOOK OF
Decorating
Hints & Tips

DK THE ULTIMATE BOOK OF
Decorating
Hints & Tips

Julian Cassell & Peter Parham

LONDON, NEW YORK, MUNICH,
MELBOURNE, DELHI

Project Editor Jude Garlick
Project Art Editor Sarah Hall
Designer Helen Benfield
Production Controller Alison Jones
DTP Designer Jason Little

Managing Editor Stephanie Jackson
Managing Art Editor Nigel Duffield

This edition published in 2009
First published in Great Britain in 1998
by Dorling Kindersley Limited,
80 Strand, London WC2R 0RL

A Penguin Company

A CIP catalogue record for this book is available
from the British Library

ISBN 978-1-4053-4936-9

Reproduced by Chroma Graphics, Singapore
Printed and bound in Singapore by
Star Standard Industries Pte Ltd.

Discover more at
www.dk.com

CONTENTS

INTRODUCTION 6

COLOUR & STYLE 10

PAINTING WALLS 22

COVERING WALLS 40

TILING WALLS 58

DECORATING WOODWORK 72

COVERING FLOORS 88

DRESSING WINDOWS 106

FINISHING TOUCHES 118

INTRODUCTION

DECORATING *can be one of the most rewarding tasks performed in the home. Hard work, creativity, and a little ingenuity can produce spectacular transformations. There are no instant means to achieving the look you desire, but there are easier methods, ways of saving time, and innovative ideas to help you. This book provides expert advice and instruction in all aspects of decoration.*

USING THIS BOOK

PREPARING TO DECORATE

Most of us realize when it is time to redecorate, but the next logical step – deciding how to do it – can be more difficult. *Colour & Style* will help you with the decision-making process by explaining the effects of combining colours and how a decorative scheme can meet your needs. The following chapters recommend essential equipment and materials, and suggest the correct preparation for the finish you desire.

Copying a motif
Use a collection of favourite items as a basis for a stencil design, as shown on page 18.

DECORATING WALLS AND WOODWORK

The walls and woodwork in a room can be thought of as a basic framework on which the rest of a room's decoration hangs. The chapter on *Painting Walls* covers all methods and techniques, ranging from the simple coverage of a wall to more spectacular paint effects. *Covering Walls* looks at every aspect of wallpapering, as well as other options such as wooden panelling. *Tiling Walls* examines the third major option for decorating walls, providing practical instruction as well as creative ideas for applying tiles to walls. *Decorating Woodwork* completes the fundamental decorative framework, providing advice on the best ways of painting woodwork, and incorporating paint effects that will completely transform the appearance of wooden surfaces – including favourite pieces of furniture.

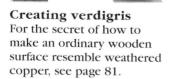

Creating verdigris
For the secret of how to make an ordinary wooden surface resemble weathered copper, see page 81.

Adding Fabrics and Finishes

The basic decorative framework of a room needs to be complemented by the rest of the room's decoration. *Covering Floors* deals with another major surface area. Whether you choose soft or hard flooring, this chapter provides many innovative ideas. *Dressing Windows* suggests some short cuts and new angles on traditional window coverings, and includes advice on decorating glass. *Finishing Touches* covers all those other items that highlight a room's decorative scheme, such as fabrics, lighting, and wall decorations, which contribute to the overall effect. Finally, the glossary provides explanations of a variety of terms that are relevant to decorating.

Looking at the whole
Plan a complete decorative look including wallpaper, borders, paints, and furnishings.

SPECIAL FEATURES

This book contains a number of special features to ensure that information is easily accessible. These include a quick-reference box at the beginning of each chapter, illustrated equipment boxes, tip boxes, warning boxes, and safety boxes, all of which are shown here.

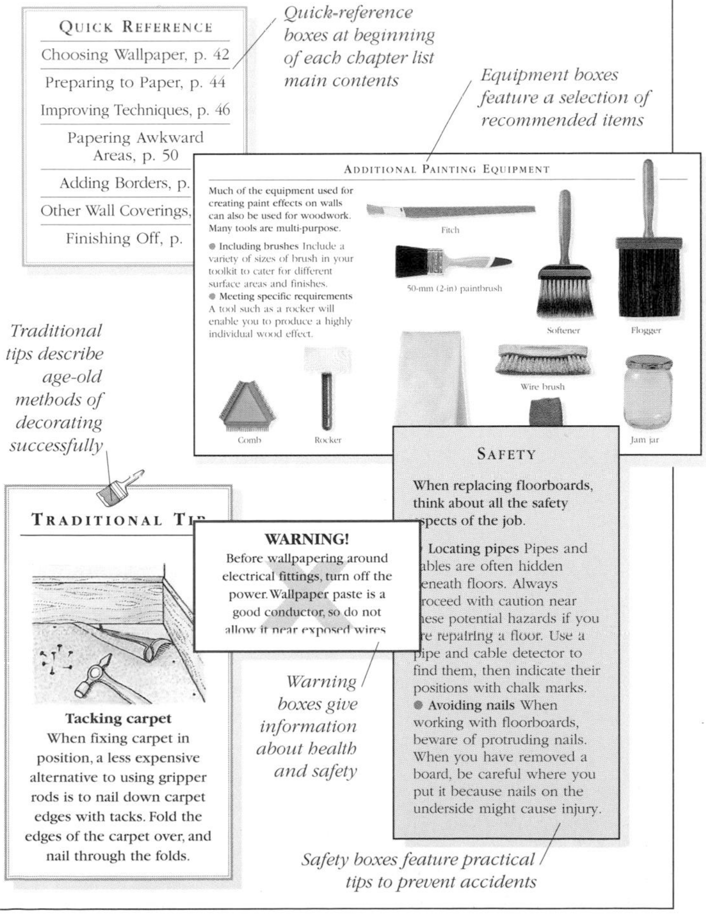

QUICK REFERENCE
Choosing Wallpaper, p. 42
Preparing to Paper, p. 44
Improving Techniques, p. 46
Papering Awkward Areas, p. 50
Adding Borders, p.
Other Wall Coverings,
Finishing Off, p.

Quick-reference boxes at beginning of each chapter list main contents

Equipment boxes feature a selection of recommended items

ADDITIONAL PAINTING EQUIPMENT
Much of the equipment used for creating paint effects on walls can also be used for woodwork. Many tools are multi-purpose.
● Including brushes Include a variety of sizes of brush in your toolkit to cater for different surface areas and finishes.
● Meeting specific requirements A tool such as a rocker will enable you to produce a highly individual wood effect.

Fitch

50-mm (2-in) paintbrush

Softener

Flogger

Wire brush

Jam jar

Comb

Rocker

TIP-BOX ICONS

Throughout this book, tip boxes highlight pieces of traditional wisdom, money- and time-saving tips, bright ideas to make decorating quick and easy, and environmentally friendly advice.

Money-saving tip

Green tip

Traditional tip

Bright idea

Time-saving tip

Traditional tips describe age-old methods of decorating successfully

TRADITIONAL TIP

Tacking carpet
When fixing carpet in position, a less expensive alternative to using gripper rods is to nail down carpet edges with tacks. Fold the edges of the carpet over, and nail through the folds.

WARNING!
Before wallpapering around electrical fittings, turn off the power. Wallpaper paste is a good conductor, so do not allow it near exposed wires

Warning boxes give information about health and safety

SAFETY
When replacing floorboards, think about all the safety aspects of the job.
● Locating pipes Pipes and cables are often hidden beneath floors. Always proceed with caution near these potential hazards if you are repairing a floor. Use a pipe and cable detector to find them, then indicate their positions with chalk marks.
● Avoiding nails When working with floorboards, beware of protruding nails. When you have removed a board, be careful where you put it because nails on the underside might cause injury.

Safety boxes feature practical tips to prevent accidents

CHOOSING THE RIGHT EQUIPMENT

Home-decorating outlets and retail chains are full of equipment designed to aid you in almost every decorating project. However, a few essential tools, together with one or two required for certain specific jobs, will arm you for most tasks. Be wary of tools making time-saving claims unless they are supported by the first-hand experience of someone you know. Quality is unquestionably the key to success when buying equipment. Remember that you can add to a tool collection as the need arises.

Making a dragging tool
Convert a car window scraper into a dragging tool by cutting "teeth" out of the blade.

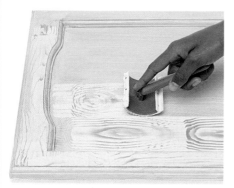

Graining wood
Use a rocker – a special-effects tool – to create the impression of a grained wooden surface.

WORKING WITH "GREEN" MATERIALS

We are constantly reminded of the need to lead our lives in an environmentally friendly way to conserve natural resources. Decorators can contribute to this ethos with relatively little effort. Materials are increasingly water based rather than solvent based. As well as being "greener", water-based products tend to be easier to use, they dry more quickly, and are much easier to clean up after use. This book recommends environmentally friendly materials and methods of cleaning up after their use, and suggests imaginative ways of using leftovers.

WORKING WITHIN A BUDGET

The amount of money that you have to spend will be an important factor when planning a decorating project. Keep your costs down by simple financial management. Always select the best materials you can afford. Good-quality paint is expensive but covers in fewer coats; underlay extends the life of a carpet; good-quality wall tiles are less likely than inexpensive ones to break when cut. Save money by long-term planning as well as short-term saving.

Using up cork tiles
Attach a few cork tiles that are left over from a flooring project to a piece of plyboard, place it inside a picture frame, and hang up for use as a home-office or kitchen noticeboard.

EXPERIMENTING WITH DECOR

Redecorating gives you the chance to experiment with different effects and finishes. A bold choice that is completely different from the existing decorative scheme can totally change the feel of a room, although a less drastic transformation may be all that is needed to revitalize its "tired" appearance. Consider several options, and experiment with ideas before you make any final decisions. Make use of colour tester pots and colour swatches from suppliers of materials and

fabrics, and practise paint effects on test areas of wall. Decorating a home can provide an outlet for your creativity and also an opportunity to channel your ideas into a practical scheme, the results of which you can enjoy for many years to come.

Trying out colours
Take home some wallpaper samples from suppliers, and look at the swatches in situ.

ENJOYING THE FINISHED PRODUCT

In a society in which many people's lifestyles have become increasingly frantic and stressful, leisure time and relaxation have become of paramount importance to counterbalance the strains of modern living. A well-decorated home can become a sanctuary from the rigours of everyday life as well as a place for relaxation and recreational activities with family and friends. A decorating project itself can provide you with an enjoyable pastime – offering the necessary distraction and relief from work and stress – and you will find successful results immensely satisfying. You will subsequently be able to relax in and enjoy pleasant surroundings that are all the result of your own ideas, planning, creativity, and – last but not least – hard work.

HEALTH AND SAFETY GUIDELINES

When decorating, consider the following important health and safety aspects.

FOLLOWING INSTRUCTIONS
● Always read manufacturers' operating instructions before using any equipment.
● Make sure that you use any materials or chemicals safely, complying with statutory legislation regulating the use of substances hazardous to health. Follow advice on labels carefully before making up solutions or mixtures.

USING EQUIPMENT
● Make sure that ladders and stepladders are in good working order, and platforms have been constructed safely, to prevent injury from falling.

DEALING WITH ELECTRICS
● Disconnect any electrical equipment when it is not in use, even for a short time.
● Switch off the power supply when decorating around switches or power points, and when cleaning them.
● Consider using a residual current circuit breaker to protect against electrocution.

PROTECTING PEOPLE
● Increase the ventilation in a room to reduce the effects of dust and fumes.
● Wear a mask to minimize the amount of dust and fine particles that you inhale.
● Wear safety glasses to protect eyes from flying debris.
● Wear gloves to protect skin from injury and irritation.
● Keep all chemicals and tools away from children, and out of the way of "corridors" within your working area.

Dust mask

COLOUR & STYLE

ONE OF THE JOYS of decorating is that it provides an opportunity to experiment with colour and decorative styles, and gives you a means of expressing your personal taste and preferences. Creating your own colour combinations and choosing styles does, however, need thought and consideration of other factors before you make final decisions.

UNDERSTANDING COLOUR

It is not necessary to understand the physics behind the derivation of colour in order to appreciate why you like particular colours or to determine a colour scheme. Rather, you need a working knowledge of how different colours are related and affect each other.

APPLYING COLOURS

● **Defining aims** Decide whether or not you want to achieve a certain result with your colour choice in a room, and the sort of mood you want to create. Select a main colour with these needs in mind – restful colours in a bedroom, for example, or warm, inviting hues in a living area.

● **Evoking emotions** Colours produce different emotional responses in people. If you want to make a statement or attract attention, use a strong, hot colour. Choose warm colours to be welcoming and comforting. Select strong, cold colours for a calming rather than a stimulating effect. Cool colours are invigorating but soothing at the same time.

● **Combining colours** Base a colour scheme around one main colour. Then consider whether other colours should form a range of consecutive hues, be clashing or contrasting complementary colours, or be combined to create a more complex scheme altogether.

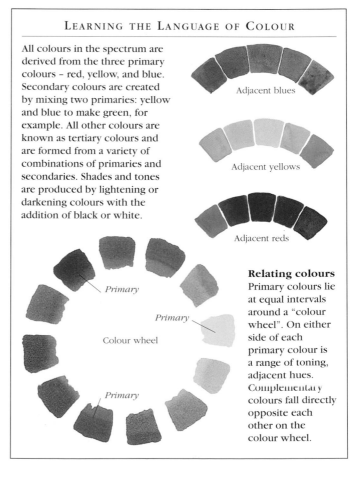

LEARNING THE LANGUAGE OF COLOUR

All colours in the spectrum are derived from the three primary colours – red, yellow, and blue. Secondary colours are created by mixing two primaries: yellow and blue to make green, for example. All other colours are known as tertiary colours and are formed from a variety of combinations of primaries and secondaries. Shades and tones are produced by lightening or darkening colours with the addition of black or white.

Adjacent blues

Adjacent yellows

Adjacent reds

Primary

Primary

Colour wheel

Primary

Primary

Relating colours
Primary colours lie at equal intervals around a "colour wheel". On either side of each primary colour is a range of toning, adjacent hues. Complementary colours fall directly opposite each other on the colour wheel.

COMBINING COLOURS

Some people have an instinctive feel for how colours combine successfully within an extensive scheme. But you can soon learn whether colours contrast with or complement each other. Either alternative can provide the basis of a highly successful colour scheme.

CONTRASTING SHADES

Juxtaposing light and dark
Using particularly light colours alongside much darker shades can provide good definition between the various surfaces in a room. Here, the light lemon of the alcove and the pale woodwork create a neat finish against dark blue walls.

COMBINING OPPOSITES

Using complementary colours
Red and green work well together because they are complementary colours – that is, they sit directly opposite each other on the colour wheel. The colour scheme featured here also includes yellow, which contrasts with the complementaries.

USING ADJACENT COLOURS

Striking a balance with related colours
Contrasting colours emphasize features, but if they are adjacent hues they also unite a room. The red walls and window link this scheme, despite a great difference in wall colours. The vibrant yellow on the skirting board contrasts with the pale yellow wall while relating to it.

CHOOSING COLOURS
● **Following instincts** Choose basic colours within a scheme according to your preferences. Once you have chosen these basics, you can make slight variations in shade to suit particular requirements.

● **Harmonizing a finish** Choose colours of the same intensity within a scheme to create a restful feel within a room. The greater the difference in intensity, the more colours will tend to stand out. You may wish to highlight a feature using this effect.

● **Mixing complementaries** Combine a large area of one colour with its complementary colour, which will have the effect of softening the original shade. You can also use this method to take the edge off vibrant hues so that they lie more comfortably together.

USING COLOUR

COLOURS HAVE CERTAIN PROPERTIES that can evoke particular feelings in a room. You may choose a colour scheme simply to change the character of your room or to create a certain atmosphere by means of that colour's characteristics.

TRANSFORMING ROOMS WITH COLOUR

When starting the decoration of a room from scratch, examine the function of the room and who is going to be using it.

● **Catering for occupants** If a room is for communal use, cater for general taste rather than individual needs. Even a personal room such as a bedroom will require very different decor, in both practical and aesthetic terms, depending on for whom it is designed.

● **Considering function** Select your colours according to whether a room will be used for rest and relaxation, for fun and recreation, or for work.

Playing with greens
In a bedroom intended for use by a child, bear in mind that its functions will include both rest and recreation. You will have the scope to use different colours to enliven the atmosphere and add interest for the room's occupant.

Relaxing in warm pinks
You can transform a room almost completely just by changing its colour. Use a uniform colour scheme in an adult's bedroom, for example, to ensure that features do not leap out and to maintain a restful atmosphere.

SUBTLE OR BOLD

Subtlety and boldness are generally equated with conservatism and daring, respectively. This is because it is considered far more risky to use bright, vibrant colours than paler hues, as brighter colours tend to have a greater initial impact and effect than more subtle variations.

STAYING PALE

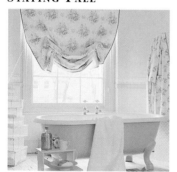

Limiting the difference
Maintain a narrow margin of difference between the colours in a scheme to produce a calming feel. The paler these colours, the more subtle the scheme, and the greater will be the effect.

BEING BOLD

Going to extremes
Use bold, vibrant colours to give a dynamic feel to a room. A bright, cheerful atmosphere can also be relaxing, and subtle lighting can create a feeling of sumptuousness and calm.

MIXING & MATCHING

● **Highlighting features** Choose subtle colours for walls, woodwork, and floors to allow you to use bold colours and patterns for soft furnishings in order to draw attention to these items.

● **Framing walls** Use bold colours on woodwork and more subtle variations on walls which will have the effect of "framing" the walls. Enhance this effect with a bold ceiling colour. The walls will then set off pictures well.

● **Using white** Include white, which is perhaps the most subtle colour of all, to show off other colours successfully.

WARM OR COOL

Colours have definite warming or cooling properties that can be used to great effect in all areas of the home. Combining several warm or cool colours, or using both warm and cool together, can produce a range of different atmospheres and moods to suit your needs.

WARMING UP & COOLING DOWN

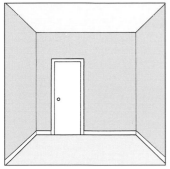

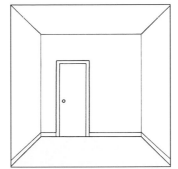

Bringing in warmth
The warming effect of these colours is enhanced by the fact that they appear to bring the walls nearer and reduce space in the room. Choose colours like these for cosiness and intimacy.

Creating space
Typical cool colours tend to have a receding effect on walls, which gives a greater feeling of space in a room. Use this to create an open, airy atmosphere, as well as creating a cool effect.

ADJUSTING EFFECTS

● **Emanating warmth** Oranges, reds, pinks, and warm yellows create a cosy atmosphere. Choose warm colours such as these for a room that receives little or no direct sunlight.

● **Freshening up** Select a cool, refreshing colour scheme with blues and greens for areas such as narrow corridors that need opening up, or for sunny rooms that may overheat.

● **Varying intensity** The extent to which a colour has a warming or cooling influence depends on its intensity and its shade. Use dark colours carefully, as these tend to have the most marked effect.

CREATING A WARM GLOW

Nurturing warmth and comfort
Create a feeling of cosiness and reassurance by basing an entire colour scheme on warm hues. In this room, the rich, red wall colour is accentuated by similar tones in the furnishings. Even the orange undertones in the natural wooden floor contribute to the room's warm and welcoming atmosphere.

KEEPING COOL

Adopting a fresh approach
Choose a colour scheme such as the all-over blues in this kitchen to provide a fresh, revitalizing feeling. In a room that is mostly used in the mornings, and which receives plenty of natural sunlight, there is probably no need to introduce warm colours to enliven the atmosphere.

LIGHT OR DARK

The use of a light or dark colour does, of course, create a correspondingly light or dark atmosphere in a room. However, different shades of the same colour have their own characteristics, and can be used individually to dramatic effect in the overall colour scheme.

MAKING LIGHT WORK

Enlarging a room
Light colours on large surfaces create a feeling of space. Use them to make a small room seem larger, or on selective surfaces such as ceilings to give an impression of greater height.

STAYING IN THE DARK

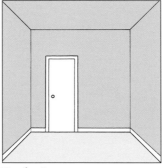

Enclosing a room
Dark colours tend to draw surfaces towards the viewer, and therefore reduce the feeling of space. Use them to "lower" high ceilings or add cosiness and intimacy to a large room.

MODIFYING CHOICES
● **Playing safe** Use light, pastel shades if you are unsure of your decorating skills. Even if you are inexperienced, you should be able to mix and match them with relative ease.
● **Covering blemishes** Dark colours, especially used on woodwork, will camouflage unevenness or blemishes better than lighter shades. Use dark colours to maximize the quality of the finish.
● **Extending life** Dark colours are better at concealing dirt and coping with general wear and tear. Choose darker shades, therefore, to prolong the life of a decorative scheme.

USING PALE COLOURS EFFECTIVELY

Keeping a room light and airy
Use pale colours to produce a very light and airy feel, as in this living room, where it is further enhanced by the use of both natural and artificial light. Maintain the continuity of these creamy tones throughout all the decorations in the room, to achieve a unified, harmonious atmosphere.

USING DARK COLOURS EFFECTIVELY

Creating warmth and cosiness
Combine relatively pale colours on the walls with contrasting, darker shades for the rest of the decoration in a room. This will produce a slightly enclosed yet at the same time very comfortable impression. Create an extra touch of opulence by making the dark colours rich and warm.

BLENDING AND TONING

Blending and toning can often be the most difficult concept to grasp when choosing colours. You have to decide which features of a room should be accentuated and which should be blended in with the general decor in order to produce a sympathetic colour scheme.

MAINTAINING A BLEND

● **Setting the tone** Choose colours to suit a room's function and the impact you wish to make. Use subtle tones in areas of rest, more intense hues in activity rooms.
● **Creating mood** Select a shade that is appropriate for a room's mood. Slightly tinting a colour one way or another can make all the difference.
● **Reducing impact** Use colours to make unsightly features less noticeable. Paint a radiator the same colour as the walls, for example.

COLOUR CO-ORDINATING

Blending together
Choose a main wall colour so that it blends in with the colour of another significant feature in the room. In the example shown here, the natural-wood finish of the fireplace and the furniture tones effectively with the pale ochre walls and smaller items such as paintings and ornaments to create a harmonious and relaxed feel in the room.

EXTENDING COLOUR

Extending the same colours and designs from one surface to another is a further way of using colour to balance a decorative scheme. This link can be made between all surfaces in a room including the flooring and furnishings, as well as the smaller decorative details.

LOCATING COLOUR IN LESS OBVIOUS PLACES

Maintaining a theme between features
Link features or rooms together by sharing a theme, for example by extending a pattern from one decorative feature to another. Here, the bands of tricoloured squares running above the kitchen work surface and above the skirting board have also been applied to the painted frame. Use constituent colours separately on other selected surfaces to echo and maintain the theme between features or rooms.

FOLLOWING GUIDELINES

● **Including ornaments** As well as using similar colours on all the major surfaces in a room, extend the colour scheme to ornaments and collections on display to co-ordinate the components of a decorative scheme even further.
● **Incorporating textures** The textured aspect of a decorative scheme can also be linked in with a colour scheme. For example, reflect the different shades and tones produced by a natural flooring, such as seagrass, in wicker baskets and other accessories in the room.
● **Scheming simply** The best effects are often created by means of a few simple colour statements. Avoid including too many colours, since this tends to produce a very cluttered feel that will be too busy for most rooms.

COLOUR SCHEMING

CHOOSING A COLOUR SCHEME is exciting, but it can also be a little daunting. You may find it easy to select a main colour but more difficult to finalize the smaller details, although these can often make or break the finished effect.

FINDING INSPIRATION

Inspiration comes naturally and easily to some people, but most of us need a little help in developing our artistic flair, or even in defining our own personal preferences. Try to identify a few pointers to help you before you start to make decisions about decorating.

LOOKING AROUND YOU

When selecting colours, you may find that inspiration is close at hand, so look around you before searching further afield.

● **Existing decorations** Examine why your existing decorative scheme does not suit you, and to what extent the colour scheme needs to be changed.
● **Magazines** Flick quickly through magazines to see which pages and images attract you, and which colours they feature.
● **Paintings** Use paintings and prints that you have bought in the past as pointers to what appeals to you visually.

Looking at photographs
Browse through a photograph album, identifying favourite holiday pictures. Make a note of those colours that appeal to you in landscape photographs, as this should give you a good idea of your colour preferences.

SEEKING HELP

● **Observing friends' homes** Although inspiration is an individual experience, you can learn a lot by looking at the colour schemes in friends' homes. Try combining ideas from several sources.
● **Consulting professionals** If you visit a decorating outlet, ask their experts for advice on colour scheming. This service is usually free and you may find it extremely useful.
● **Visiting showrooms** Most large outlets build lifesize showrooms to display entire schemes. Observe the work here of interior designers.

TRADITIONAL TIP

Using colour charts
Many manufacturers now provide more than simple colour swatches to aid your choice of colours. They will also advise on period colour styles and how to combine colours to create an authentic look. Many of their materials have traditional finishes.

STARTING OUT

● **Trying technology** There are many computer programs available to help with home design and decoration. You can try out a range of different colour schemes on screen before making any decisions or doing any practical work.
● **Considering lighting** You need to be aware of the lighting in a room, since this will affect colours. Study both natural light conditions and artificial lighting before selecting a colour scheme.
● **Choosing accessories** Pick out the decorative accessories for a room before selecting a colour scheme, concentrating on objects that you particularly like or find inspirational.

USING SWATCHES

Painting lining paper
Make a reasonably sized colour swatch by painting a piece of lining paper. Stick this on a wall temporarily so that you can observe a colour as the light changes throughout the day.

BUILDING UP A COMPLETE DECORATING SCHEME

Choosing the decoration of a room from scratch can provide an exciting challenge and thus be very rewarding on completion. From the starting point of a chosen colour or several colours, follow through to every last detail of decorative materials, furnishings, and ornamentation in the room.

Choose fabrics for upholstery and window dressings that highlight one or combine several of the colours in your decorative scheme

Select bowls and other ceramic ornaments so that they reflect the colours you have chosen

Pick out combinations of colours – in this case blue and pale terracotta – from holiday photographs that you particularly like

Look through books on painting or photography for ideas on using and combining colour and tone

Use carpet samples to select appropriate shades to co-ordinate with the colours of other decorative materials and complete your chosen colour scheme

Make a much-loved ceramic pot the anchor point for colour scheming, or buy a new item specifically for that purpose

Try out paint on a wall using samples – which are available in small quantities – before making a final decision about colours

SETTING STYLES

WHEN PLANNING A DECORATIVE SCHEME you need to decide whether to follow an established style or create your own look. A combination of both is possible, with many permutations allowing you to be as creative as you wish.

FORMING IDEAS

As with colour scheming, look for additional inspiration from various external sources when choosing a decorative style. Balance a number of different ideas carefully to achieve a result that you will be happy with, and which will also be appreciated by other people.

DECIDING ON STYLE
● **Verifying age** If you wish to give your home a period look, do some thorough research into the requisite colours and styles before beginning work.
● **Watching films** Watch films and television productions as a source of inspiration and reference. In their need for authenticity, producers – especially of period dramas, for example – have to pay great attention to detail.
● **Keeping existing style** If you are happy with an existing style, you may need simply to update or renew it. Do not feel obliged to change a look each time you redecorate.

KEEPING WITHIN BUDGET
● **Decorating lavishly** Consider the costs of reproducing a particular style. Extravagant drapes may be needed for a period look, for example. You will then have to cut back on other expenditure, such as that for decorative accessories.
● **Making structural changes** Costs rise if major structural work is carried out. Decide whether or not the benefits of the work will justify the additional expense incurred.
● **Choosing paint** Paint is less expensive than wallpaper or other materials. Adapt a style to include painted surfaces for a less costly option.

DOING RESEARCH

Source material for planning your style can be found in a number of different locations. All of these may inspire you and help you to form your ideas before decision-making.

● Exhibitions.
● Libraries.
● Magazines.
● Illustrated books.
● Craft fairs.
● Lifestyle and home-decorating programmes.
● Theatres.
● Trade shows.
● Art galleries.
● Museums.
● Places of historical interest.

BRIGHT IDEA

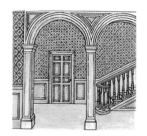

Viewing period homes
Seek inspiration for original styles from period homes. Visit a few, particularly locally, to get a feel for the character of the region and note inspirational elements.

USING COLLECTIONS

Use a personal collection as a basis for a theme, extending its appeal and making it a significant part of a room's decoration.

● **Using furniture** Some people collect furniture that reflects a particular historical period or influence. Use this theme as a basis for other decorations by matching colours and designs to complement the pieces.
● **Using pictures** Decorate a room so that your pictures will be enhanced by their surroundings. Large paintings can usually cope with lavish wall coverings, whereas smaller prints need a subtler backdrop that will not compete with them.

Stencilling a design
Copy an image from an item that is displayed in the room – part of a collection, for example – by tracing over it. Use this to create a stencil design which, as well as adding decorative appeal to the wall, will also complement the item or collection.

CONSIDERING OTHER FACTORS

When setting a style there are a number of supplementary considerations that you need to take into account in order to achieve an authentic effect. These factors may not be obvious, but can help you to make the practical decisions that will shape the final scheme.

BEING LAVISH

● **Using the right fabric** Lavish, sumptuous styles rely heavily on soft furnishings. To create this sort of feel, emphasize elaborate window dressings, extravagant furnishings, and the impression of swathes of material and cushions, as well as soft, luxurious carpeting.

THINKING AHEAD

● **Considering your stay** If you will not be in a home for long, cater for short-term needs, and avoid extravagant decor that you will have to leave behind.
● **Increasing value** Make sure that your home is decorated well. It will be far easier to sell – and fetch a higher price – when the time comes.
● **Dealing with trends** Decorative styles change as quickly as other fashions. To play safe, choose a fairly neutral scheme, and reflect fashion only in accessories.

CREATING FORMALITY

● **Being ordered** Formal styles can range from opulence to minimalism. However, designs for wallpaper or fabric should be precise and obvious to give an impression of regimented order. For example, choose striped designs for a neat, tidy, and ordered appearance.

MINIMIZING CHANGES

● **Following a design** Massive overhauls are not necessary to inject the idea of a style into a decorative scheme. Select fabrics carefully for immediate effect. Gingham designs, for example, suggest a country-cottage feel, even if used relatively sparingly in a room.

CONSIDERING BUILDING STYLES

A particular decorative scheme will work better in some surroundings than in others.

● **Reflecting reality** Consider authenticity. For example, a country-kitchen look is most convincing in a rural setting.
● **Maintaining a theme** When decorating part of your home, think about the impact on other areas, and whether you will extend the style to them later. If a finish reflects a particular era, changing it may mean replacing other decorative features too.

Reflecting architecture
Certain types of building are best suited to particular styles of decor. A look that works well in a Hispanic-style villa may be out of place in a town house or a rustic, wooden home.

TRANSFORMING A SPACE INTO A LIVING AREA

Starting from scratch
For a major room facelift, or the creation of a living area in previously unused space, clear the room as much as possible. Here, a cold, uninviting room (above) has become welcoming and comfortable (right), and good use has been made of inherent features such as its unusual shape and natural light.

REFLECTING LIFESTYLES

W HEN MAKING DECISIONS ABOUT DECORATING, consider your lifestyle as well as your feelings about how living environments should appear. You may be constrained by architectural features, but there are many ways to adapt them.

SELECTING A STYLE

A ll decorators are, in effect, presented with a blank canvas on which to work. When planning your creation, you will need to strike a balance between a look you like and the functions a room will serve. First resolve basic requirements, then make adjustments to style.

LIVING IN AN URBAN ENVIRONMENT

Maximizing space

Space may well be at a premium if you live in a town dwelling. Consider an open-plan layout to help create a feeling of greater space, or simply to make the most of the space that you have available. Light colours are more likely than dark shades to make a room feel spacious, especially if it has high ceilings. Think very carefully about the layout of and furnishings for an open-plan home. It can be challenging enough to co-ordinate the decoration of a small area, let alone take a creative overview of a large room that has to serve multiple purposes. So take your time when making choices.

DESIGNING A COUNTRY KITCHEN

Recalling the simple life

Choose a country look for a kitchen to reflect a theme of uncomplicated living and promote comfort and relaxation in one of the busiest areas of the home. Reinforce this atmosphere by using a lot of wood, both painted and unpainted.

REFLECTING A REGIONAL STYLE

Adding an ethnic flavour

You can develop a theme with just a few details, or create a complete replica of a regional style – be it local or from far afield. This Hispanic theme is simply produced with a little basic knowledge about the appropriate colours and designs.

SELECTING A MODERN OR A TRADITIONAL APPROACH

Being thoroughly modern

Modern decorative schemes are often characterized as much by their selection of furniture, such as these striking chairs, as by their colour scheme and choice of fabrics. A modern style is innovative, so you can give yourself scope to experiment and produce a style that reflects your own ideas.

Upholding tradition

Many people feel comfortable with traditional decorative themes, like the classic look of this room. Tried and tested over the years, such styles are to a certain extent guaranteed to give a satisfying result. You can choose from a wide range of options and are likely to find a selection to suit your taste.

CREATING A HOME IN ONE ROOM

Planning a room layout carefully

When one room is to be used for a number of purposes, design the decor largely according to practical concerns. Here, split-level accommodation creates space by suspending the sleeping area above ground level. The choice of a few ornate accessories, such as the mirror and the pillar support of the raised area, adds interest.

MAKING YOUR MARK

- **Adding to a look** There is no need to complete your decorative scheme as soon as the main decorating job is completed. Collect and add accessories and ornaments over time until you feel you have achieved a total look.
- **Creating a focus** The most successful decorative schemes result from well-chosen focal points that draw attention to detail. Fireplaces, furniture, and pictures all fall into this category. However, do not clutter up a room and reduce the impact of such features. Minimalist decorative schemes draw attention to focal points.
- **Adapting a style** Take an established style and adapt it to suit you. This can be great fun and will add a touch of individuality. For example, include an extravagant material in a Shaker-style kitchen to contrast with the simple, utilitarian designs.

PAINTING WALLS

WALLS AND CEILINGS are usually the largest surface areas that you will paint in a home. As a result, wall colour and texture form the backdrop for other decoration in a room. It is therefore important to prepare surfaces thoroughly and use the correct technique for the finish required to ensure both the quality and long life of the decoration.

SELECTING MATERIALS

There is a vast and ever-increasing variety of painting materials in the marketplace, but they broadly fit into a number of general categories. Water-based paints tend to dominate the wall-finish market because they are quick-drying and easy to use over large surface areas.

PAINT TYPES AND THEIR CHARACTERISTICS

TYPE	FINISH	USES	COVERAGE
Matt emulsion	Water-based, dull matt; easy to work with and low-odour therefore user-friendly.	All walls and ceilings; particularly suitable for new plaster since allows it to dry out thoroughly.	16 m²/litre (87 sq yd/gal)
Vinyl matt emulsion	Water-based, wipeable matt; more hard-wearing than ordinary matt emulsion.	All walls and low-wear areas; matt properties help to conceal many surface imperfections.	16 m²/litre (87 sq yd/gal)
Vinyl silk emulsion	Water-based, high sheen; very practical since wipeable and even washable.	All walls and ceilings; particularly suitable for kitchens and bathrooms since easy to clean.	15 m²/litre (82 sq yd/gal)
Proprietary flat emulsion	Water- or oil-based, dead flat matt; several makes available with slight finish variations.	All walls and ceilings; ideal for achieving a traditional, flat paint finish.	16 m²/litre (87 sq yd/gal)
Eggshell	Oil-based, medium sheen; some are low-odour and therefore more user-friendly than others.	All walls and ceilings, but particularly suitable for high-wear areas.	16 m²/litre (87 sq yd/gal)
Quick-drying eggshell	Water-based acrylic, medium sheen; some are impregnated with fungicides.	All walls and ceilings; hard-wearing, low-odour, and quick-drying properties.	15 m²/litre (82 sq yd/gal)
Textured	Water-based thick matt; can be left plain or painted, and can have pattern superimposed.	All walls and ceilings; hard-wearing and covers poor surfaces and cracks well.	5 m²/litre (28 sq yd/gal)

BASIC PAINTING EQUIPMENT

Having the most suitable tools for painting projects is very important. There are several basic tools that should form part of every home decorator's painting kit, and which may then be added to for tasks with more specific requirements. Buying good-quality equipment will reap benefits in the form of better, longer-lasting results.

● **Creating paint effects** If you intend to use paint effects, you will require some additional equipment as well as certain different materials (see p. 31).
● **Testing equipment** Before buying any painting equipment – but especially large, costly pieces – test them for sturdiness, and make sure that they have an adequate guarantee.

Fitch

50-mm (2-in) brush

100-mm (4-in) brush

Smooth roller sleeve

Rough roller sleeve

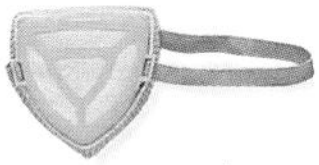

Dust mask

Tape measure

Paint kettle

Roller cage

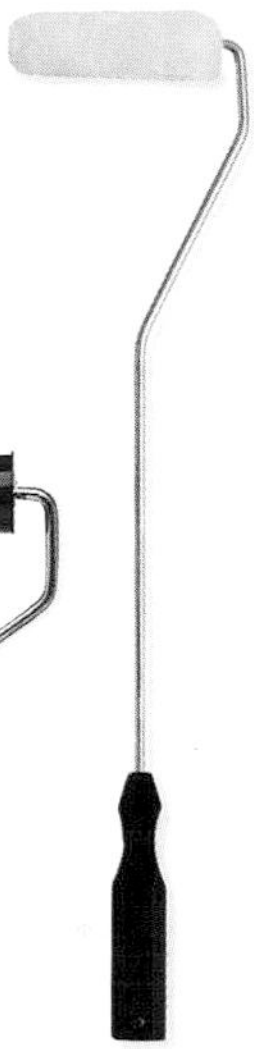

Radiator roller

Roller extension handle

Bucket

Dust sheet

Roller tray

Filling knife

Sandpaper

MEASURING UP

Accuracy when estimating the amount of paint you require for decorating will save you money and produce less wastage. Once the appropriate areas have been measured, use the chart opposite as a guide to rates of coverage in your calculations of paint quantities. These rates have been worked out assuming walls have average porosity.

● **Walls** Calculate the surface areas of walls simply by multiplying the height of a room from the ceiling to the top of the skirting board (or to the floor) by the entire length of the skirting board (or the perimeter of the floor).

● **Ceilings** To calculate the surface area of a ceiling, use the dimensions of the floor.
● **Doors and windows** Do not subtract the areas of doors or windows from your calculations. This means you will have enough paint left over for any touching up that may be necessary at a later date.
● **Extras** Make sure that you allow a little extra paint for items such as coving, wall or window recesses, pillars, covered beams, and alcoves.
● **Coverage** Most walls will require two coats of paint. Usually, the second coat will need only 80 per cent of the paint required for the first coat.

SAFETY

Consider the following safety recommendations before you begin a painting project.

● **Preventing injury** Ensure that you store materials and tools away from children and pets. Many products contain chemicals that can cause irritation to the body.
● **Following instructions** Read all manufacturers' guidelines with regard to the proper use of materials and equipment before using them.
● **Climbing safely** Inspect all ladders and stepladders carefully to make sure that they are safe to use and show no serious signs of wear.

PREPARING TO PAINT

THE FIRST STAGE OF THE DECORATING PROCESS is important to the production of a top-quality finish, but it is often perceived as the most tedious. Taking time to prepare a wall thoroughly before painting will ensure a good result.

MAKING SURFACES READY

Protecting surfaces that are not to be painted is as important as preparing those that are. It is advisable to remove all furniture from a room to protect it from damage, to increase your working area, and to make it easier to identify those areas of wall needing most attention.

CLEARING & COVERING

● **Protecting furniture** If it is not possible to move all the furniture out of a room, stack large items in the centre of the room and fit smaller pieces around them. Drape a plastic sheet over the furniture to keep dust off. Secure around the bottom with masking tape.
● **Covering floors** Cover floors with decorators' dust sheets or old household sheets. Use a double thickness of the latter as they are less impermeable.
● **Stopping movement** Secure dust sheets by skirting boards with masking tape to prevent them from "creeping".

FILLING WALLS

● **Mixing filler** Mix filler to a firm, paste-like consistency. Too wet and it will shrink too much in a hole when it dries; too dry and it will be difficult to work and dry too quickly.
● **Storing prepared filler** If you prepare too much filler, store the surplus – covered with clingfilm – for later use.
● **Filling large gaps** Use newspaper to pack out corner cracks and provide a base for filler. Deep holes will need a second fill before sanding.
● **Filling proud** Fill holes slightly proud of the wall surface to allow for shrinkage.

REPAIRING CORNERS

Using a support
To repair an external corner, nail a batten flush with one edge, and fill against it. Once the filler dries, remove the batten. Repeat on the other edge, and lightly sand.

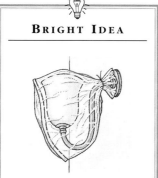

BRIGHT IDEA

Protecting fittings
To protect a wall fitting such as a light from paint splatters, cover with a plastic bag secured with string. Remove the light bulb which, if switched on, would heat up and present a fire risk.

COVERING LARGE AREAS

Using a caulking blade
If a wall has numerous scrapes and holes, use a caulking blade to spread filler across the whole or a large part of the damaged area. The broad blade surface will cover the area efficiently.

MAKING ALTERATIONS

● **Putting up coving** Strip old wallpaper before attaching new coving to walls. Fix coving in position before doing any further painting preparation.
● **Replacing woodwork** If you want to replace architraves or skirting boards, do so before you paint the walls in order to avoid the possibility of them being damaged after they have been painted.
● **Organizing professionals** Hire qualified tradespeople to carry out any major electrical or plumbing alterations that are necessary before you start painting. Arrange for them to return once you have finished the decorating to complete the second fixings for you.

PREPARING WALLS

A smooth wall surface is essential, since paint highlights rather than hides imperfections. Sand excess filler and other rough areas back to a dead flat finish that is smooth to the touch. Prime with an appropriate sealer to stabilize the surface and make it ready to accept paint.

SANDING & SEALING
● **Sanding large areas** Use an electric sander for preparing large expanses of wall. Hiring one for a day is not expensive.
● **Maximizing use** Once coarse sandpaper has become worn, you can use it for fine sanding before throwing it away.
● **Sealing new plaster** Dilute ten parts of matt emulsion with one part water for use as an excellent primer on new plaster. Choose white emulsion since it is the least expensive.
● **Sealing dusty walls** Mix one part PVA with five parts water to make an excellent sealer. It will have strong bonding properties and be ideal for using on powdery walls.

MAKING SANDING EASIER
● **Saving time** Before sanding, remove lumps of plaster or filler with a scraper. Only a light sand will then be needed for total smoothness.

Fold sandpaper around wood

Using a sanding block
Wrap a piece of sandpaper tightly around a wood offcut to provide a firm base as you sand a wall. Rotate the sandpaper around the block as it wears

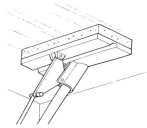

CLEANING DOWN

Clean a ceiling thoroughly before you start painting it.

● **Reaching a ceiling** Rather than climbing a ladder with a bucket of water, use a squeegee mop to reach up.
● **Using detergent** Use a mild detergent for cleaning, then rinse with clean, warm water.

PREPARING PAINT

Paint will produce the finish that you require only if it is prepared correctly before you use it. Problems such as poor colour matching, shadows, and a poor finish are usually not the fault of the paint manufacturer but more often the result of poor preparation by the user.

MIXING PAINT
Stir with batten

Maintaining colour
You may require several cans of paint when decorating a large room. Pour all of them into one large bucket and mix to conceal colour differences. Use a bucket with an airtight lid for storage.

REMOVING LUMPS
Pour paint into paint kettle through sieve

Sieving paint
However well it is stored, paint may form a skin in the can or acquire lumps and foreign bodies. Use a household sieve when decanting paint into a paint kettle to separate out these impurities.

STIRRING & DECANTING
● **Protecting paint** Before opening a can of paint, always use a soft brush to remove dust and dirt from the rim of the lid. Impurities may otherwise fall into the paint as you ease off the lid.
● **Hand stirring** Stir paint in several different directions rather than in a one-directional movement. Use a slight lifting motion as you stir to ensure an even colour throughout and the dispersal of paint up from the base of the can.
● **Lining paint kettles** Use foil to line a paint kettle before decanting paint into it. Once the job is finished, the foil can be thrown away and there is no need to clean the kettle.

IMPROVING TECHNIQUES

As YOUR PAINTING TECHNIQUES IMPROVE, you will achieve the desired finish efficiently and accurately. You can cover large areas quickly with modern equipment. Never rush, and remember that speed will come with practice.

IMPROVING THE BASICS

Even if you have a preference for a particular technique, it is worth experimenting with alternative methods. You may be surprised to find that a technique that you had previously considered to be difficult is, in fact, easier than you thought and well within your capabilities.

FOLLOWING BASIC RULES

- **Smoothing walls** Rub down walls lightly between coats with fine-grade sandpaper.
- **Lighting efficiently** Paint with an indirect rather than a main light source illuminating your work. You will then be able to see more clearly where you have painted, especially on the second or third coat.
- **Keeping edges wet** Keep the edge wet as you paint along a wall, since differing drying times on the same surface may cause shading variations. Complete one wall at a time.
- **Covering well** Apply two coats if you are making a slight colour change, but three if you are replacing dark with light.

LOADING PAINT

- **Filling trays and kettles** Fill a tray up to the bottom edge of its ribbed slope, and a paint kettle up to one-third full.

Distributing evenly
Run a roller head over the ribbed area of a paint tray to remove excess paint. This will also ensure that the paint is evenly distributed over the roller head.

TRADITIONAL TIP

Dampening brushes
Dampen paintbrushes before use to make them easier to work with. Wash your brushes regularly during painting to prevent the bristles from clogging up. Dampen rollers and pads, too.

SELECTING BRUSHES

Using brushes efficiently
Choose a 100-mm (4-in) brush for painting walls. Using a smaller one will take too long, while a larger one will cause your wrist to tire. Apply random strokes in all directions, and do not overbrush. Lay off as with a roller.

ROLLERING WALLS

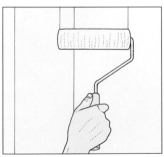

Covering evenly
Apply paint on a roller in vertical, slightly overlapping strips. One load should cover 1 m² (1 sq yd). Without reloading, lightly run the roller over the area to lay off the paint, removing excess and producing an even coverage.

USING PAINT PADS

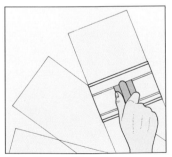

Painting with ease
Using a paint pad requires a minimal amount of technical ability. Prevent a build-up of paint by spreading it in all directions, but make sure that all areas within the range of the pad are sufficiently covered.

PAINTING AROUND EDGES

Painting around the edges of a wall is known as cutting in, and requires great precision. Good defining lines between different surfaces will add a touch of professionalism to your decorating. Usually a brush is used, although corner rollers and miniature pads are available.

DEALING WITH EDGES

● **Overlapping** Cut in a little way on to architraves and skirting boards if they are to be painted. Then you will only have to paint one straight line – when you paint the woodwork.
● **Masking** If you are painting walls but not woodwork, apply a strip of masking tape along adjacent wooden edges. Do this also if you intend to apply a natural wood finish.
● **Painting around switches** Use a fitch to cut in carefully around switches. Clean off oversplashes when they are dry with the edge of a filling knife or a window scraper.
● **Painting inaccessible areas** It is hard to paint between pipes and behind radiators. Use a long-handled radiator roller, or make a tool by taping a sawn-off paintbrush at a right angle to the end of a dowel.

PAINTING A WELL-DEFINED EDGE

● **Choosing brushes** Use a 50-mm (2-in) brush to paint in a corner. This will be small enough to manoeuvre, but will cover a reasonably sized area with a single loading of paint.

● **Hiding unevenness** Where the edge of the ceiling is undulating, cut in slightly below the wall–ceiling junction to produce a new line that is clearly defined and straight.

CUTTING IN AT A WALL–CEILING JUNCTION

1 Apply a strip of paint along the top of a wall between 2.5 and 5 cm (1 and 2 in) below the ceiling. Do not brush this trail out, and apply a thicker covering of paint than you would if you were painting the open wall.

2 With the brush now mostly unloaded of paint, spread the paint trail upwards right into the wall–ceiling junction. Using the outermost bristles, bead the paint accurately into the corner, making a clean, straight line at the junction.

ADAPTING TECHNIQUES FOR PAINTING CEILINGS

Slight modifications in painting techniques are required when painting ceilings because of the difficulty in reaching them. You will need a sturdy stepladder. When decorating a whole room, make sure that you paint the ceiling first, thus preventing overspray on to walls that have already been decorated.

● **Increasing your height** If you find stepladders cumbersome, and you have low ceilings, you may be able to paint a ceiling merely by standing on an upturned wooden crate.
● **Dealing with light fittings** Unscrew ceiling roses rather than trying to paint around them. Make sure that the electricity supply is turned off first.

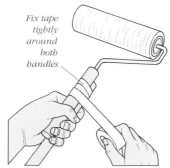

Fix tape tightly around both handles

Staying on the ground
Reduce the amount of work you have to do up a ladder when painting a ceiling by using an extension pole with a roller or paint pad. If you do not want to buy an extension pole, improvise by taping a roller or paint pad to one end of a broom handle.

● **Overlapping walls** If walls are to be painted, overlap ceiling paint 5 cm (2 in) on to the wall. You will find it is easier to cut in the wall colour than the ceiling colour at the junction of the two.
● **Protecting from overspray** If you are not using a drip guard, protect yourself from spray by wearing a long-sleeved shirt and a cap, or use non-drip paint.
● **Making a drip guard** Cut a washing-up liquid bottle in half vertically. Attach one half to a roller cage by screwing the cage's retaining screws through holes at ends of the bottle. When you roller, any paint spray will be caught by the guard. You may have to modify the design and method of attachment for different brands of roller.

USING EQUIPMENT

Technological developments continually bring new painting equipment and tools into the marketplace and improve existing decorating methods. Paint sprayers, for example, are more suitable for use in the home than they used to be, and are readily available for purchase or hire.

EMBRACING TECHNOLOGY

● **Reducing effort** Use battery-powered rollers and brushes to eliminate the need for reloading. Paint is pumped through a tube on to the roller or brush head, thus speeding up the painting process and making it easier.

● **Improving coverage** Use proprietary one-coat paints to reduce significantly the time it takes to decorate a room. These paints are ideal for partial redecoration and for freshening up a room quickly.

● **Buying multipurpose tools** These days manufacturers produce tools with far more than their traditional purpose in mind. Combination ladders, for example, have a number of uses – as trestles and working platforms as well as conventional stepladders.

CHOOSING TO PAINT WITH A SPRAYER

● **Spraying with ease** Hand-held, airless spray guns are light and relatively easy to use. Practise on a piece of newspaper. Clean the nozzle regularly for an even coating.

● **Following guidelines** Apply several even, thin coats for a dead flat finish: thick coats make paint more likely to run. Spraying can be messy, so mask off bordering surfaces.

Maintaining a steady hand
With one hand in control of the trigger, use the other to steady the sprayer. Keep the nozzle about 30 cm (12 in) from the wall. Wear lightweight gloves to protect your hands from overspray.

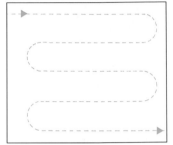

Covering a wall
Spray in a continuous motion, backwards and forwards across a wall and from top to bottom. Spray a little way beyond each wall edge. Keep spraying until the wall is completely covered.

SAFETY

As with any equipment, read manufacturer's instructions carefully when using a paint sprayer. There are particularly important safety points to remember with sprayers.

● **Wearing protective clothing** Wear a mask and goggles when using a paint sprayer. Never inhale the fine mist of paint or get it into your eyes.

● **Protecting hands** Never put your hands in front of a sprayer's nozzle. The paint is expelled at high pressure and could cause injury.

● **Disconnecting power** Always disconnect a paint sprayer from the power supply before you remove the nozzle – when clearing blockages, for example.

CHOOSING PAINTING TOOLS

TOOLS	CHARACTERISTICS AND SUITABILITY
Brush	Brushes are multi-purpose and come in many shapes and sizes. They are ideal for cutting in and painting intricate details, and can be used on open wall surfaces, but will be slower than other tools.
Roller	Rollers are ideal for wide open surfaces, being by far the quickest tools for covering walls efficiently. Their size varies, but rollers are too large for cutting in. The texture of rollers also varies.
Sprayer	Sprayers are ideal where little masking is required, and for painting broad wall surfaces and inaccessible areas such as behind pipes. Using a sprayer can be a messy business, so protect adjacent surfaces.
Pad	Pads are suitable for large surfaces, and small pads are available for cutting in. They cause less mess than rollers. Use them where extensive masking would otherwise be necessary, such as in kitchens.

EMPHASIZING TEXTURE

Greater depth and texture can be produced by applying specialist coatings and paints to wall surfaces. These finishes look effective and are almost as easy to apply as more conventional paints. Their thick formulation means that they literally add another dimension to your painting.

MAKING PATTERNS

Using tools
Use a small grout spreader to create a design. Work in areas of about 1 m² (1 sq yd) or the paint will dry before you have made the pattern. A semi-circular shape is easy to reproduce if you want to keep the design relatively simple.

DEALING WITH CORNERS

Cutting in
Use a small stippling brush to apply paint in corners, since a textured roller will not reach right in. Dab lightly with a well-loaded brush to achieve the rough finish produced by a textured roller on an open wall.

LEAVING WALLS LOOKING NATURAL

Many wall surfaces provide a textured or natural look in their own right. This requires minimal additional finishing.

● **Natural stone** Seal natural stone with a coat of diluted PVA (one part PVA to five parts water). This will provide a finish, while the bonding properties of the PVA-based sealer will reduce dust.
● **Brick** Use proprietary watersealers to give bricks a low-sheen finish that is attractive and functional.
● **Bare plaster** A well-plastered room can itself be pleasing. Seal with two or three coats of water-based matt varnish.

APPLYING SPECIALIST COATINGS TO CEILINGS

Specialist coatings designed with ceilings in mind can provide effective finishes. They are ideal for areas that are prone to cracking, or for uneven ceilings that need to look more uniform. As with textured paint, you can create a wide variety of patterns with tools designed specifically for the task, or, by improvising with different implements, you can create your own individual look.

● **Getting help** Try to find someone to help you with the application of a textured coating to a ceiling, since it is a difficult job to do on your own. One of you can apply the coating, while the other follows behind creating the pattern.
● **Cleaning as you go** Keep a bucket of clean water to hand as you texture a ceiling. Rinse your tools regularly in the water to prevent them from becoming clogged up with the coating.
● **Finishing edges** Frame a finished ceiling by dragging a 25-mm (1-in) brush through the textured coating all the way around the perimeter. This will create a precise, well-defined edge to enhance the finish.

Removing drip tips
Once a textured coating is dry, gently brush the ceiling with a household broom to remove any excess coating. Otherwise, when you paint the ceiling, rollers will catch on the drip tips, hampering an even paint distribution.

Creating effects
Use a crumpled plastic bag to create a textured effect. Turn the bag regularly so that you use a clean area to make the imprint. Wear surgical gloves to prevent your hands from becoming caked, and keep some bags to hand.

CREATING PAINT EFFECTS

Y̶OU CAN CREATE A WIDE RANGE OF EFFECTS by using paints and glazes. Use paint for designing patterns and deceiving the eye with colour and perspective. Use glazes for their semi-transparent quality to produce depth and translucence.

CONSIDERING OPTIONS

Simple paint effects can have just as much impact as those involving more complex techniques. If you are a beginner, choose a simple effect that uses coloured emulsions. You can mix coloured glazes, and attempt more extravagant finishes, as you gain experience.

CHOOSING EFFECTS
● **Selecting methods** There are two main methods of creating paint effects. Either a tool is dipped into paint or glaze and then applied to a wall, or a glaze is applied to a wall with a brush and a tool is pressed into the glaze. The former is an "on" technique; the latter is "off". Even if you use the same glaze and the same tool, a different finish will be achieved depending on which method you employ.
● **Applying a base coat** Always apply a base coat. Light shades are best, since you can then build up colour: eggshell or emulsion are ideal.

PREPARING TO PAINT
● **Roughing it** Examine all walls carefully. Rough, textured walls are ideal for sponging, which disguises defects, while smooth, dead flat walls will show stippling off to its best.
● **Assessing suitability** Choose ragging or bagging rather than rag rolling on a wall that has pipework or switches. Rag rolling needs a constant motion, not frequent interruptions. Joins are difficult to disguise.
● **Getting ready** Make sure that all materials and tools are ready for use, since once you start a wall you should finish it without interruption. If you do not, some areas will dry before others and the joins will show.

TYPES OF PAINT EFFECT

Whichever paint effect you choose, make sure that you have all tools and materials to hand. Try to maintain consistent hand movements from one wall to another for an even overall finish.

Sponging on
Sponging (see p. 32) is probably the easiest paint effect to create. Emulsions or glazes can be used. Natural sea sponges are the ideal tools to work with, although synthetic sponges can be substituted.

Sponging off
A mixed glaze should be used for this effect (see p. 32). A sea sponge must be used since substitutes tend to smudge the finish. This is a natural progression from sponging on in terms of difficulty.

Ragging
Ragging (see p. 33) involves a similar technique to that of sponging, except a crumpled, lint-free cloth is used instead of a sponge. A mixed glaze should be used for the best results.

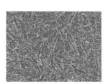

Bagging
Bagging (see p. 33) involves the same technique as ragging, except a plastic bag is used instead of a rag. This creates a more sharply defined texture compared to the fabric alternatives used in ragging.

Rag rolling
With rag rolling (see p. 33), a rag is rolled down the wall to create the effect of tumbling material. It is best to rag roll off, since uniformity and consistency are difficult to achieve when applying on.

Stippling
A stippled effect (see p. 32) is created by pressing the bristle tips of a stippling brush into a wet glaze. The technique is only suitable for glazes, and continuity is important to prevent joins or overlaps.

ADDITIONAL PAINTING EQUIPMENT

Building up a paint-effect tool kit can be expensive, so do it gradually. Buy equipment as you need it, rather than purchasing everything that you think you may need in the future, only to find that you use few items.

● **Improvising** You can use tools other than special-effect equipment for paint techniques. Experiment with different objects – ordinary household items as well as decorating tools – to create unique effects.

Large decorating brush

Flogger

Lint-free cloth

Stippling brush

Masking tape

Stencilling brush

Natural sponge

Craft knife

Plastic bag

Cutting mat

COLOURWASHING

Colourwashing is probably the oldest paint technique. Use a large paint brush to apply a highly diluted glaze to wall surfaces. This will produce a translucent finish through which the base coat shows, creating depth and texture.

● **Stabilizing a wash** A wash should have the consistency of highly diluted paint. To prevent it from running off the walls, add a small amount of PVA to the mix to help it adhere to the wall surface.
● **Adding depth** Apply several coats and vary colour slightly to create a wonderful feeling of depth. Warm colours will give a glow to any room.
● **Choosing walls** Apply a wash to a rough surface to create texture. The colour will clear from the peaks but build up in the troughs, creating a great textured finish.

MAKING GLAZES

A glaze is the medium for creating paint effects. It is distinguished by its ability to hold patterned impressions and long drying time that allows you to create an effect. Glazes have traditionally been oil based, but modern acrylics are popular and are often supplied ready mixed.

COLOURING GLAZES

Mix colours before adding to glaze

Mixing acrylic colours
Use an artist's brush to mix acrylic colours. Mix the colour first on a surface such as a paint-tin lid, and make sure it is the right shade. Decant the basic glaze into an old jam jar, and add the acrylic colour to it.

CALCULATING QUANTITIES

● **Diluting colour** For a good acrylic-based glaze, five to ten per cent of the mixture should be colour and the rest glaze. Add the colour to the glaze and mix thoroughly. A clean jam jar is ideal for mixing small quantities of colour in this way, since you can screw the lid on tightly before shaking the colours to mix them well.
● **Estimating amounts** Glazes go much further than standard paints. Dilute acrylic glazes with a small amount of water to increase the coverage of the glaze. Estimate how much you will need by halving the amount of standard paint you would require to cover the same-sized area of wall.

TRADITIONAL TIP

Mixing a traditional glaze
For 1 litre (1¾ pt) add 600 ml (1 pt) white spirit to 300 ml (½ pt) boiled linseed oil and 120 ml (⅕ pt) white, oil-based undercoat or eggshell. Tint using artist's oil paints.

SPONGING

Whether sponging whole walls or selected areas, such as beneath a dado rail, this effect transforms the look of a flat wall surface. A single layer of sponging produces a subtle, airy pattern, while multiple layers produce a busier, bolder effect that has greater depth.

SPONGING SUCCESSFULLY

● **Removing excess** When sponging on, decant the glaze on to an old plate or rimmed paint-tub lid. Dip the face of a damp sponge into the glaze, and remove excess by drawing the sponge across the rim, otherwise the first impression will be thick and blotchy. If you do apply too much, reapply some base colour.
● **Rotating the hand** Rotate the hand into a slightly different position after each impression to keep the pattern random.
● **Sponging corners** Tape a small piece of sponge on to the end of a pencil to enable you to reach right into corners.

USING COLOUR EFFECTIVELY

Sponging dark on to light
Use a light base coat and gradually apply darker shades on top to produce a highly distinctive pattern. The colour of the final coat applied will always be the most dominant.

Sponging light on to dark
Use a dark base coat and apply progressively lighter shades on top for a translucent effect. You will see a larger colour range since the light colours will not obliterate preceding coats.

STIPPLING

Stippling is a subtle paint effect, using a brush to create the impression of a textured surface that may range from a light, velvety appearance to a coarser finish, depending on the size and compactness of the bristles. This is a time-consuming technique, but very satisfying.

CHOOSING BRUSHES

● **Using specialist brushes** If you can afford one, buy a stippling brush, which is ideal for stippling since it consists of a thick wad of bristles.

Finding an alternative
For a less costly alternative to a stippling brush, trim the bristles of a wallpaper-hanging brush with sharp scissors. Make a dead flat pad of bristles so that all the ends will be in contact with the wall.

STIPPLING EFFECTIVELY

● **Working in sections** Apply glaze in areas of about 1 m² (1 sq yd), using a large paint brush. Cover as evenly as you can, then dab the stippling brush lightly on the wet glaze.
● **Creating uniformity** Work from left to right and top to bottom. Do not overlap stipples because they will appear as more heavily shaded areas.
● **Preventing clogging** After each area has been stippled, wipe the head of the brush with a lint-free cloth to remove excess glaze. A build-up of glaze will create a patchy effect over the wall.
● **Adding depth** Use a slightly darker glaze in the corners of a wall than towards the centre to create a feeling of depth.

TIME-SAVING TIP

Glazing with a roller
Use a fine mohair roller to apply glaze to a wall. This is much quicker than using a brush and therefore allows more time for creating an effect. Do not overload the roller, or the glaze might run.

RAGGING

Ragging is similar to sponging, except that a crumpled lint-free cloth is used rather than a sponge. Ragging "off" (see p. 30) is easier and more effective than ragging "on". With the latter, cloths become clogged up with glaze, producing a rather gummy, patchy finish.

CREATING THE EFFECT

Building up pattern
Using a damp, scrunched-up rag, apply light pressure on the glaze. Change your grip frequently to produce a random pattern. Return to missed areas before the glaze dries. Rinse the cloth regularly.

SHIELDING SURFACES

Avoiding smudges
Hold a strip of card against the adjacent wall to prevent the edge of the rag from smudging colour on to it. Move the card down as you paint. Wipe the card regularly to avoid a glaze build-up.

BAGGING

Use the same technique as for ragging, but substitute a plastic bag for the lint-free cloth.

● **Choosing bags** You will need a ready supply of bags to hand so that you can throw one away and pick up a new one as you need to.
● **Experimenting** Different types of plastic create different effects: do not be afraid to experiment.
● **Softening edges** Bagging creates an angular effect. For a more understated look, gently brush the bagged surface. Use a softening or wallpaper-hanging brush.

RAG ROLLING

Rag rolling requires a more ordered technique than simple ragging, because the effect created is one-directional: it mimics falling material. It is ideal for areas such as those beneath dados and in wall panels, since it is difficult to execute uniformly over large areas.

ROLLING SUCCESSFULLY

● **Choosing rags** Make sure that your rags are all cut to the same size, and made of the same material. The pieces should not include seams.
● **Applying glaze** Apply the glaze in strips from top to bottom of the area to be ragged. Make each strip slightly wider than the rolls.
● **Dealing with corners** You need both hands to roll a rag down the wall, making it impossible to shield adjacent walls. Make sure that you mask the nearest 15 cm (6 in) of the adjacent wall with newspaper and masking tape.
● **Combining techniques** Stipple the glaze before rag rolling to create a softer, more material-like effect.

PREPARING RAGS

● **Having supplies to hand** Roll up a number of rags before you begin to create this paint effect, and keep them close at hand once you have started.

Keep rag rolls together in paint tray

Making lengths consistent
Tie off the ends of the rags so that the central portions are of a consistent size. Keep them in a paint tray to prevent them from picking up dust, which would then be transferred to the walls.

IMPROVING TECHNIQUE

Maintaining uniformity
Start rag rolling in one of the top corners of the area to be covered to establish a straight edge all the way down. Overlap each length of rolling slightly, so as to make a continuous pattern.

CREATING STRIPES

Stripes are commonly associated with formality and a sense of order within a room. Creating your own stripes gives you lots of scope to design highly original patterns and use colour effectively. Choose imaginatively when it comes to equipment and methods of application.

USING A CHALK LINE

Ensuring that lines are straight is very important in decorating. Use this traditional technique to mark out lines in readiness for painting stripes.

● Snapping a line Measure and mark off the widths of the stripes along the top of the wall. At each mark, knock in a 2.5-cm (1-in) nail up to about half its length, having checked that there are no pipes or wires beneath the surface. Hook a chalk line over the nail, and pull taut to the floor, making sure that it is vertical. Gently pull the chalk line away, and snap it against the wall to create a chalk impression. Remove the nail, and repeat the process at the next mark.

MARKING OUT STRIPES
● Chalking lines Buy powdered chalk (contrasting with the wall colour) to fill a chalk-line reservoir, or rub a stick of chalk along a piece of string.

Masking off areas
Run masking tape down the chalk guidelines before painting. Secure firmly the edge adjacent to the area to be painted: leave the other edge loose for easy removal. Use a soft brush to dust away the chalk before painting.

STRIPING FREEHAND
● Rollering stripes Masking guidelines can be a long job: save time by settling for a less exact finish. Use a masked roller – preferably a foam one.

Using a masked roller
Wrap two pieces of 2.5-cm (1-in) masking tape tightly around a 17.5-cm (7-in) roller. Load with paint and roller the wall, creating the striped effect. Use the right-hand stripe as a guideline to align the roller for the next run.

ROLLERING PATTERNS
● Varying stripes Extend the technique of creating stripes using a roller to include all kinds of patterns within the stripes. Create different designs by modifying the roller itself.

Cut-out areas do not pick up paint

Using a patterned roller
Use a craft knife to cut diamond shapes, for example, out of a foam roller sleeve before use. Apply paint from a tray in the usual way: the diamond-shaped "holes" will not pick up paint and create a pattern on the wall.

MAKING A CHECKED PATTERN

Combine horizontal and vertical stripes to produce a pattern of checks similar to that of gingham. The colour that you use for the horizontal stripes should be lighter than that used for the verticals. This will create a third colour at the crossover points.

1 Use a long spirit level to keep the stripes vertical. Move the level down the wall each time you reload the roller. Work from right to left so that the level does not smudge stripes that have been painted.

2 Allow the vertical stripes to dry thoroughly. Use the level horizontally to paint the top layer of stripes. Work from the top downwards. The stripes may have uneven edges, but this adds to the material effect.

STENCILLING

This technique allows you to reproduce a design or pattern accurately over a surface as many times as you like. Stencils can be made up of a single sheet or a number of superimposed layers. The latter option creates depth and allows you to use different colours.

USING STENCILS

● **Loading brushes** Cover the ends of the bristles evenly, but only with a minimal amount of paint. Remove excess on paper before applying to the wall. Too thick a coverage of paint will make it seep under the edges of the stencil.

● **Holding in place** Keep a stencil in position on a wall with masking tape. Low-tac tape will not pull the base coat off when the stencil is moved.

● **Mixing colour** Stencils offer an excellent opportunity to mix and vary colours. Create subtle differences in shade from one area to another to produce a mellow, aged effect.

● **Keeping stencils clean** Wash acetate stencils regularly in warm water to keep their edges clean and free of paint.

CREATING DEPTH

● **Using shading** To lend a three-dimensional effect to a stencilled image, vary the degree of shading across it.

Shading around edges
Make the colour intensity greater around the edges of a design. To add more depth, shade one of the edges slightly more, creating an impression of shadow and hence directional sunlight.

CHOOSING AN IMAGE

● **Getting ideas** Use books and magazines as inspiration. Make sure that the image you choose has a distinct outline and clear detail within it.

TRACING & CUTTING A STENCIL

Cutting mat

1 If you make an acetate stencil, you will not need to trace an image first. Secure acetate over an image with masking tape, and trace outline and detail with a wax crayon.

2 Cut the stencil carefully so that it has smooth lines. You will use one stencil to create many images, so make a good job of it. Use a cutting mat if you are cutting a lot of stencils.

PLACING DESIGNS

● **Stencilling a border** Use a spirit level and a soft pencil to draw a continuous line all around the walls about 30 cm (12 in) from the ceiling, having measured the correct drop at several points around the room. Sit the bottom edge of the stencil on this line, and follow the line around with the stencil, thus creating an attractive border. Do not forget to rub out the pencil line carefully with an eraser once you have finished.

● **Grouping images** Follow through a theme by grouping images together. Animals are a popular subject for this treatment. Three leaping dolphins in a bathroom, for example, or a collection of farmyard animals in a kitchen can look very effective.

SELECTING TOOLS

● **Cutting stencils** Use a craft knife, ideally with a narrow handle for easy manoeuvring. Cut stencil edges at a slight angle to limit paint seepage.

FINDING ALTERNATIVES TO A BRUSH

Experiment with other implements for stencilling instead of a stencilling brush to produce a range of effects.

● **Sponging** Use a natural sea sponge to create a highly textured stencilled effect.

● **Crayoning** Try special stencilling crayons or traditional crayons. Ensure that the end of the crayon is very rounded, and use it in a circular motion.

● **Spraying** If you are using aerosol paints, which are ideal for stencilling, mask all around the stencil with newspaper to prevent overspray beyond the image.

● **Improvising** Cut down the bristles of an old paintbrush to make a stencilling brush.

PRINTING

Printing offers an alternative to stencilling in transferring a painted image on to a wall. It need not be an exact science, and you can use a variety of tools. Stamping and blocking are the techniques: an image stands proud on a stamp; with a block it takes up the whole surface area.

PRINTING EFFECTIVELY

● **Stamping** Buy ready-made stamps or make your own by cutting a design into a small piece of linoleum. Glue a wooden block to the back of the lino to act as a handle. Load paint on to the face of the stamp with a rigid mini roller.

● **Blocking** Use household objects such as sponges or potato halves to make a block. These sorts of "tools" are readily available in the home and achieve a good texture.

● **Increasing depth** Vary texture by stamping or blocking on to a piece of paper before applying the tool to the wall, to reduce the density of paint.

USING STAMPS

Rolling on to a wall
Place the bottom edge of a stamp on the wall, and roll it on to the wall until the top edge makes contact. Hold for a second, then lift off carefully. This motion will ensure a crisp, clean impression.

CHOOSING BLOCKS

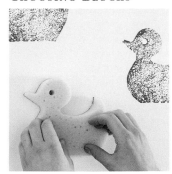

Making a block
Transfer a shape on to a household sponge, and cut it out with sharp scissors. Place the sponge fully on to the wall and agitate it slightly without changing its position. Reload frequently.

CREATING MURALS

Producing a mural is not as daunting as you may think; it is simply another method of transferring a drawn or copied image on to a wall. Some artistic ability is helpful but not essential, since – in its simplest form – this technique is no different from painting by numbers.

USING AN IMAGE OF YOUR OWN CHOICE

● **Selecting an image** Choose a subject that suits the nature of the room in which it is to appear, and that is not too detailed and difficult to copy.

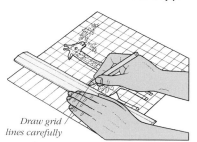

Draw grid lines carefully

1 Secure some tracing paper over an image. Measure out and draw an accurate grid so that it covers the picture. A grid made up of 2.5 cm by 2.5 cm (1 in by 1 in) squares is a standard workable size.

2 Scale up the grid on to the wall using chalk or a soft pencil. Using the first grid as a guide, fill in the corresponding squares on the wall. Erase the chalk dust or pencil lines when you have finished.

SAVING TIME

● **Projecting a design** Use a slide or overhead projector to transfer a design directly on to a wall. Adjust the size by moving the projector closer to or further away from the wall.

● **Painting quickly** Have a selection of different-sized brushes to hand, so that you will have the right size for the area you are painting.

● **Painting with a steady hand** Hold one end of a 45-cm (18-in) length of dowel with your non-painting hand, and place the other end against the wall (make sure it is padded to prevent it from scratching the paintwork). Rest the forearm of your painting arm on the central section of the dowel to maintain a steady hand.

DECEIVING THE EYE

Paint can be used to create all sorts of different illusions on a flat surface. These illusions vary greatly in complexity, and many of them require a lot of time and care to execute. Simple applications, however, can often prove just as effective as more extravagant ideas.

CREATING THE IMPRESSION OF STONE BLOCKS

1 Paint the whole wall with a light base colour. Mark out block shapes with strips of 1-cm (½-in) masking tape. The masked areas will be the mortar lines in the finished effect.

2 Sponge on two coats that are darker than the mortar colour. Apply the second before the first has dried, so that the colours merge. Apply lots of paint for texture. Allow to dry.

3 Remove the masking tape to reveal the mortar. For a weathered effect, mix burnt umber with a little yellow ochre, and paint some cracks with a fine-tipped artist's brush.

PAINTING INTERIOR SURFACES TO LOOK LIKE EXTERNAL WALLS

● **Increasing texture** Use coarse-grained, exterior masonry paint for the base coat to add texture and create effective mortar. You can add sand to interior emulsion for a similar effect.

● **Varying colour and texture** Choose paint colours according to the type of surface you wish to mimic. Apply using a fibrous sea sponge to achieve a more finely textured finish.

● **Being authentic** Increase realism by enhancing the outlines of shapes with a soft pencil. Darken the edges to add depth. Do this before removing the masking tape.

INCLUDING *TROMPE L'OEIL* IMAGERY IN YOUR DECORATING

Technically, painting stonework is *trompe l'oeil*, but the term is more commonly associated with the reproduction of specific objects on a wall. Such images appear three-dimensional and therefore seem life-like.

● **Keeping it simple** If you are a beginner, do not be too bold. Recreating a life-sized kitchen cupboard, for example, would test the most experienced decorator. Small items such as picture frames are a good start.
● **Mixing real with false** This will often produce the most realistic *trompe l'oeil*. For example, paint in a decorative cord between a vertical row of hanging plates or pictures.

Painting flat surfaces
Producing an illusion of depth on a flat surface is not easy. Paying attention to small details, however, will add considerably to the realism of the effect. Paint an illusory cabinet in the same style as the real furniture in the room.

Using an alcove
Alcoves provide an opportunity to paint *faux* shelves. The depth of the recess adds yet another dimension to the effect. Here, real items are hung alongside imaginary ones to help bring the whole picture to life.

FINISHING OFF

THERE ARE A NUMBER OF FINAL TOUCHES that can enhance the finish of any painting project and smooth the way for future work. Once you have finished, make sure that you clean equipment thoroughly and store it it well.

PREVENTING AND CORRECTING MISTAKES

It is almost inevitable that you will have some problems with your painted surfaces – most resulting from inadequate preparation or poor technique. Many can be corrected with only a little amount of extra work, which is well worth doing in order to enhance the overall finish.

DRYING PROPERLY
- **Avoiding patches** Not allowing paint to dry out fully before recoating may produce a shadowed or patchy finish. In such a case, leave for 24 hours, and apply another coat.
- **Speeding up drying** In a cold room or one prone to damp, reduce drying time by heating the room. Otherwise paint may wrinkle or discolour.

REMOVING OVERSPILL
- **Cleaning fittings** If paint gets on to electrical fittings, remove it very carefully when dry using a scraper or filling knife.
- **Dealing with woodwork** Wall paint on woodwork need not be a problem if the woodwork is to be painted. Sand back pronounced drips or areas of roller spray.

DEALING WITH CRACKS
- **Settlement cracking** The appearance of cracks in wall surfaces soon after painting usually indicates movement of the building. This is common in new houses as settlement occurs. Redecorate affected areas when movement ceases.
- **Prolonged cracking** Persistent movement because of climate, the age of the building, or the installation of heating can be more of a problem. Consider using flexible proprietary paints and fillers, or lining the walls to cover hairline cracks.

RECTIFYING PAINT FAULTS

There are various common paint faults that can haunt decorators. Most can be solved with relative ease, and few necessitate a fresh start. Use a fine-grade sandpaper when repairing a top coat.

Poor coverage
This is the simplest of mistakes, resulting from not enough paint or too few coats being applied. Recoat the area, being sure to load equipment correctly and spread the paint using the appropriate technique.

Brush marks
Brush marks may remain visible on the painted surface once they are dry. Small areas may be acceptable on the grounds that they create a traditional feel, but larger areas should be sanded back and recoated.

Roller trails
Roller trails are caused by not laying off the paint during application, and allowing too much paint to gather at the roller edges. Carefully sand back the affected area, and touch in carefully with a brush.

Flaking paint
Paint is likely to flake if it has been applied to an unsealed, dusty wall. Sand the affected area right back until the flakes have been removed, stabilize the surface with a proprietary sealer, then recoat with paint.

Assorted stains
There are a number of miscellaneous stains, resulting from rust spots for example, that may show through a top coat. Cover the area with an oil-based undercoat or primer, allow to dry, and repaint with top coat.

Drip marks
Drip marks on a painted surface occur when paint has been applied too thickly, and therefore begins to sag or run down before it dries. Sand back the affected area, and touch in with top coat using a small brush or fitch.

CLEANING AND STORING EQUIPMENT

Keeping equipment clean ensures that it will be in good working order the next time you want to use it, and that it will not deteriorate more quickly than it should. Efficient and ordered storage makes it easy to find items and work out your requirements for future projects.

CARING AFTER USE
● **Conserving water** Most wall paints are water-based, so you can wash brushes and other painting equipment under a running tap. Remove excess paint on newspaper first, thus reducing the amount of water required for cleaning, and limiting the amount of paint entering the water supply.
● **Washing brushes** Massage a small amount of household detergent into the bristles of brushes to speed up cleaning. This will also make the bristles softer and more flexible when you come to use them next.
● **Preventing rust** After cleaning metal items such as roller cages and paint trays, make sure that you dry them thoroughly with a soft cloth, otherwise they may rust.
● **Recycling paint cans** Wash out paint cans thoroughly when you have finished with the paint, and use for storing a variety of household items.

STORING BRUSHES

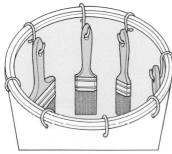

Hanging brushes
Hang brushes from hooks around the inside of a can or bucket. (Dry any damp bristles first with a hairdryer, otherwise they will stick together.) Stored in this way, bristles will be protected from the risk of being crushed.

CLEANING THOROUGHLY
● **Using a scourer** If you do not clean a paintbrush well after you have finished using it, paint will accumulate at the base of the bristles and on the ferrule, and the brush's life will be considerably reduced.

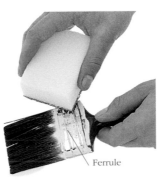

Ferrule

Scouring a ferrule
Clean off dried-on or stubborn paint from ferrules and brush handles using a kitchen scourer. You can also use a scourer on the bristles but only lengthways, otherwise the bristles will splay out and lose their shape.

STORING MATERIALS
● **Keeping paint** Store paints inside the house if possible. They can be adversely affected by temperature fluctuations. Hold lids on firmly and shake cans to produce an airlock to prevent a skin from forming.
● **Storing glazes** Write the recipe for a glaze on the side of the jar in case you want to mix more at a later date.
● **Caring for stencils** Store stencils between pieces of card and somewhere flat, such as in a book. Stencils can only be reused if they sit flat.
● **Storing dust sheets** Launder sheets before storing, or they will spread dust next time.

DISPOSING OF PAINT
● **Protecting the environment** Never dispose of decorating materials down sinks or drains. Pour all paint leftovers into one can, secure the lid tightly, and dispose of it with the rest of the household waste.

BRIGHT IDEA

Labelling paint cans
Always label cans after decorating, noting which room of the house they were used in, and on what date. Use self-adhesive labels or strips of masking tape.

REMOVING PAINT

However carefully you place dust sheets over a floor and fasten them down with masking tape before you start decorating, some paint splashes may find their way on to the carpet. Deal with them promptly and effectively.

● **Using a craft knife** Allow the paint to dry completely, then scrape across the surface with a craft knife. Hold the blade at right angles to the floor so as not to cut into the carpet. The paint will gradually crumble, and you can then remove it with a vacuum cleaner.

COVERING WALLS

THE MOST COMMON ALTERNATIVE to painting walls is wallpapering. More innovative decorators may alternatively like to use fabric in a similar way to wallpaper. For a solid, traditional finish, various types of wooden panelling, which may be painted or left natural, can be used. The many wall-covering options make it easy to select a finish to suit your practical and economic needs, as well as satisfying your personal preferences.

SELECTING WALLPAPERING MATERIALS

Wallpapers are manufactured in a number of finishes. Prices vary greatly, and the most expensive wallpapers are not necessarily easy to hang, however aesthetically pleasing they are. There is a wide choice of inexpensive wallpapers, and they are usually easy to hang.

WALLPAPER TYPES AND THEIR CHARACTERISTICS

TYPE	FINISH	USES
Lining	Undecorated, smooth, off-white or buff-coloured wallpaper. Available in different grades of thickness.	Ideal base for painting and wallpapering; suitable for all areas of the home. Disguises blemishes well.
Woodchip	Undecorated, rough-textured, off-white or buff-coloured wallpaper. Coarseness of wallpaper varies.	Excellent for covering walls and ceilings that are in poor condition; suitable for all areas of the home.
Embossed	Thick-textured wallpaper with relief-imprinted patterns. Produces a three-dimensional finish.	Wide choice of pattern available so suitable for any room. Heavyweight wallpaper so difficult to use on ceilings.
Standard decorated	Flat wallpaper with a motif or pattern that has been machine-printed on to the surface of the wallpaper.	Highly decorative and excellent for use in bedrooms, but not suitable for high-wear areas of the home.
Flock	Fibrous-material finish attached to backing paper. Synthetic-fibre make-up.	Creates a rich, sumptuous feel, so ideal for formal drawing or dining rooms.
Vinyl	Vinyl is a flat, decorative wallpaper with a clear, protective vinyl coating. Blown vinyl is embossed, with a protective vinyl layer, and is attached to backing paper. Heavy-duty vinyl is a thick, decorative paper with a protective vinyl coating.	Vinyl's wipeable surface makes it suitable in all rooms. Blown vinyl is more hardwearing than standard embossed paper, and hides blemishes well. Heavy-duty vinyl is ideal for kitchens and bathrooms since it can often be scrubbed.

BASIC WALLPAPERING EQUIPMENT

You will need more equipment for papering walls than for painting. Many tools, however, are required for both, so once those items are in your toolkit they can be used for either job.

● **Prioritizing quality** Buy the best-quality tools that you can afford. This is particularly important for the items that are used most, and those that come into direct contact with the wallpaper, such as wallpaper-hanging and pasting brushes, seam roller, scissors, and a craft knife. The latter two items are vital for making accurate cuts and, therefore, achieving the best possible finish.

● **Choosing brushes** Select a pasting brush that will cover a surface evenly and efficiently, and a wallpaper-hanging brush with long, flexible bristles.

● **Considering safety** Follow the same safety precautions with regard to wallpapering materials and equipment as for painting (see p. 23).

Goggles

Wallpaper-hanging brush

Pasting brush

Rubber gloves

Pasting table

Pencil

Cross-head screwdriver

Slot-head screwdriver

Wallpaper-hanging scissors

Seam roller

Filling knife

Ruler

Spirit level

Bucket

Chalk line

Steam stripper

Wallpaper scraper

Sponge

Stepladder

Craft knife

Measuring jug

Tape measure

CHOOSING WALLPAPER

T HE SHAPE AND USAGE OF A ROOM, the style of your home, and any effect that you wish to achieve are factors to bear in mind when choosing wallpaper, but whether or not you like a wallpaper will have most influence on your choice.

CONSIDERING EFFECTS

If you want to achieve a specific effect in a room, the decisions that you make about pattern and design can be as important as your choice of colour. A desire to create the illusion of space, for example, may influence you as much as a wallpaper's other decorative qualities.

WEIGHING UP OPTIONS
● **Hiding defects** Choose a textured or heavily patterned wallpaper to detract from uneven walls. A busy pattern will disguise a problem best.
● **Creating order** Use bold, geometric designs if you want to create a sense of order and formality within a room.
● **Using two wallpapers** If a room has a natural dividing line, such as a dado rail, use two different wallpapers to combine effects, to create a feeling of height, for example.
● **Considering other colours** Bear in mind the colours of walls and woodwork when choosing wallpaper. It should be complemented by nearby colours to maximize its effect.

CO-ORDINATING DECOR
● **Creating a total look** Buy a complete range of decorative materials so that fabrics, wallpaper, and paint match.

Matching accessories
Use matching wallpaper and fabric to create a co-ordinated look. Tie in other accessories by picking out different tones of the colours used in the wallpaper.

CREATING HEIGHT

Using stripes
Vertical stripes make a room look taller, and are ideal if ceilings are low. Here, a room divider covered in striped wallpaper contributes to the illusion of height.

CHOOSING LARGE PATTERNS

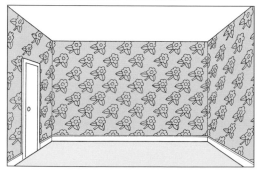

Reducing the size of large room
A large pattern can dominate the decoration in a room, since it will seem to bring the walls towards a viewer, reducing the feeling of space. In a small room a large pattern can be overpowering, but in a big room it can help to create a cosy feel.

CHOOSING SMALL PATTERNS

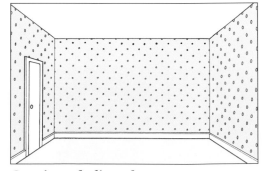

Creating a feeling of space
A small pattern has the effect of making a room appear larger, as long as the background colour of the wallpaper is pale. The less dense the pattern, the greater the effect. A dense pattern, even if it is small-scale, creates a busy feel within a room.

PLANNING THE WALLPAPERING

I t is vitally important to work out how much wallpaper is required for a room, and to determine the order in which the room will be wallpapered. Measure walls accurately so that there will be no wastage, and think carefully about where in the room to start wallpapering.

MEASURING THE DIMENSIONS OF A ROOM

● **Measuring total surface area** Measure each wall as a separate entity. Add together wall areas, plus the ceiling area (obtained by measuring the floor), to give the total surface area.

● **Including repeats** To account for trimming and wastage of large-patterned wallpaper, add the depth of the pattern repeat to the room height. This will guarantee enough wallpaper.

CALCULATING ACCURATELY

● **Including lining** If you want to line the walls of a room before wallpapering them, remember to include lining paper in your calculations of material requirements. Lining paper has no pattern repeat, so the surface area alone is all you need for the calculation.

● **Doing a quick count** In a room that is already papered, count how many hangs were used before. This is a quick way to measure the number of rolls of wallpaper that you will need. In rooms of average height, small-patterned paper gives four hangs per roll, while large-patterned paper gives three. Most wallpapers conform to a standard roll length.

● **Wallpapering ceilings** Wallpaper a ceiling in the direction of its longest length. This will keep the number of lengths required to a minimum as well as reducing trimming and the wastage of wallpaper.

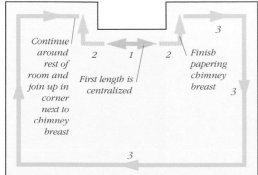

Multiply height by width of wall

Do not deduct door (or window) areas from calculations to allow for trimming and wastage

Measure floor area instead of ceiling

Calculating quantities
Multiply the height of a wall by the width (1 x 2) to calculate the surface area. Measure the height in several places, since it may vary. To obtain a ceiling measurement, measure the floor (3 x 4). Divide the total surface area by the area of a roll of wallpaper to give the number of rolls required for the room.

STARTING & FINISHING IN THE CORRECT PLACE

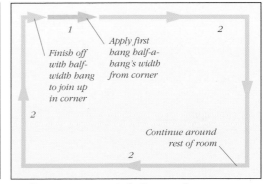

Continue around rest of room and join up in corner next to chimney breast

First length is centralized

Finish papering chimney breast

Finish off with half-width hang to join up in corner

Apply first hang half-a-hang's width from corner

Continue around rest of room

Centralizing the first hang
If using a large-patterned wallpaper in a room with a focal point such as a chimney breast (1), start by centralizing the pattern on the focal point (see p. 49). Finish the focal point (2) before continuing to wallpaper around the rest of the room (3).

Wallpapering straightforward rooms
In rooms where no centralizing is required, start wallpapering near the corner that is least visible when entering or sitting in the room (1). Make sure that the first hang needs no complicated trimming and is a good point from which to continue (2).

PREPARING TO WALLPAPER

A CERTAIN AMOUNT OF PREPARATION is necessary prior to wallpapering, depending on the finish you want and whether or not the walls have been papered before. Wallpaper faults are not always easy to put right, so prepare surfaces well.

STRIPPING WALLS

Strip all old wallpaper before hanging a new wallcovering. Some manufacturers suggest that you remove only the top layer of vinyl wallpapers and use the backing layer instead of lining paper. This is only possible, however, if that backing layer is stuck firmly enough.

STRIPPING EASILY
● **Stripping dry** Remove any loose wallpaper before soaking to reduce the amount of mess caused by water and wet paper. Where seams have lifted, you can get a good hold. Vinyl top layers usually pull away easily.
● **Soaking walls** Use hot water to soak wallpaper. Apply the water with a large pasting brush. Leave it to penetrate for a few minutes before removing the wallpaper with a scraper.
● **Protecting floors** Stripping is messy, so you need to protect the floor. As well as dust sheets, put rolls of newspaper at the bases of walls to soak up water run-off.

SCORING WALLS

Making your own scorer
Adapt an old roller head by inserting long screws at regular intervals so that they protrude out of the other side. Run the roller over the wallpaper to pierce it and so allow water to reach the paste.

TRADITIONAL TIP

Using vinegar
Add a small amount of vinegar to hot water to make a potent stripping agent. The vinegar will react with wallpaper paste, loosening it.

SAFETY

When using a stripper, wear goggles to protect your eyes, and keep out of the way of the hot steam. You may wish to protect your hands with gloves.

● **Following instructions** Read the manufacturer's guidelines carefully before using a steam stripper, since one machine may differ from another.
● **Leaving unattended** Turn a stripper off when not in use.
● **Stripping ceilings** Beware of hot water droplets that can collect on the edge of the pad and drip on to you.
● **Keeping cables dry** Ensure that no water comes into contact with electrical cables.

USING A STEAM STRIPPER

Steam stripping is by far the most effective way of removing wallpaper from walls. Hiring a steam stripper is not expensive, but consider buying one if you intend to strip a lot of wallpaper throughout your home.

● **Filling a stripper** Fill a steam stripper with hot water, not cold, to reduce the boiling time required. The equipment will then be ready to use sooner.
● **Checking water levels** Make sure that a steam stripper always has plenty of water in it. If you allow the stripper to boil dry, you may damage the element, which will necessitate some expensive repairs.

Stripping effectively
With one hand holding the stripper pad in position against the wall, use the other hand to scrape off the wallpaper where the pad has just been. Soaking times will vary depending on the type of wallpaper.

PREPARING WALLS

Whether walls have just been stripped or are being wallpapered for the first time, good preparation is vitally important. Filling and sanding are essential. Some wallpapers may disguise wall imperfections, but a good surface is necessary for paper and paste adhesion.

DOING THE BASICS

● **Providing a key** Sand glossed walls or those with a silky smooth finish to provide a key for wallpaper adhesion. This will also speed up drying: paste will dry "into" the wall and "out" through the paper.

● **Sealing dust** Seal dusty surfaces with a coat of size or a PVA solution (five parts water, one part PVA). This will help wallpaper to stick but allow you to move it easily.

● **Covering texture** If you cannot remove a highly textured coating with a steam stripper, apply a stabilizing coat of diluted PVA (five parts water, one part PVA), then coat the surface thinly with plaster.

HIDING IMPERFECTIONS

● **Masking stains** To prevent stains from bleeding through and discolouring wallpaper, spray the affected area with a proprietary stain-blocking agent, or apply an oil-based primer before wallpapering.

● **Removing protrusions** Take old nails and screws out of the wall with a claw hammer, or knock them in and fill. Make sure they are well beneath the surface to prevent staining.

● **Covering dark backgrounds** When applying light-coloured wallpaper to a previously dark or patchy wall, apply a coat of light emulsion to even out patches and prevent the dark colour from showing through.

TIME-SAVING TIP

Filling and sizing
Fill any small holes. Before the filler dries, cover the area with a PVA solution (five parts water, one part PVA). Carefully smooth it with a brush to eliminate the need for sanding.

PREPARING AND PAPERING CEILINGS

As with most decorating jobs, it is best to start at the top and work down. Ceilings should be tackled first after all standard preparation has been carried out.

● **Filling edges** Ensure that the wall–ceiling junction is precisely filled and sanded, since this edge will provide the guideline for wallpapering on both the ceiling and the walls.

● **Testing ceilings** Old emulsioned ceilings may be unstable. The weight of wallpaper may pull the paint off, causing the wallpaper to sag. Apply a small test patch of wallpaper to the ceiling, and leave it overnight. If it is still firmly stuck in the morning, continue wallpapering.

● **Playing safe** If you are unsure about the stability of a ceiling, strip off the old paint with a scraper before proceeding any further. Then prepare the surface and seal as usual.

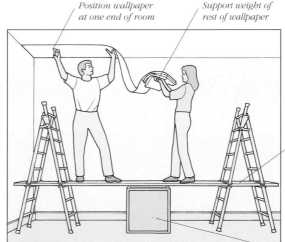

Position wallpaper at one end of room

Support weight of rest of wallpaper

Plank supported at end across open stepladder

Plank made sturdy by support of box in middle

Working safely and easily
Build a sturdy work platform by suspending a plank between two stepladders. Support the plank with a wooden box. Adjust the height of the platform so that the ceiling is about 15 cm (6 in) above your head – close enough to allow you to move the wallpaper easily, without being cramped. Ask a friend to help you to hold a length of wallpaper while you apply it, to reduce the risk of tearing.

IMPROVING TECHNIQUES

Tℍᴇʀᴇ ɪs ᴏɴʟʏ ᴏɴᴇ ᴛᴇᴄʜɴɪϙᴜᴇ for applying wallpaper to a wall – with a paper-hanging brush and various trimming tools. The secret of success lies in the preparation of the surface and your ability to wallpaper around obstacles.

═══ MEASURING AND CUTTING ═══

Accurate measuring will ensure that there is minimal wastage in what is inevitably a wasteful technique. Before unwrapping and cutting wallpaper, check that all the rolls have the same batch number, thereby avoiding the possibility of colour variations between rolls.

STARTING OUT
● **Making equipment ready**
Make sure that scissors are sharp and that the surface of the pasting table is clean before you start work.
● **Measuring walls** Measure the exact distance between the ceiling and the top of the skirting board. Add the depth of the pattern repeat, plus 10 cm (4 in) for trimming.
● **Stacking hangs** Most hangs will be of a standard length within a room. Cut a number of these lengths to start with, so that you have them to hand when you need them.

WORKING WITH PAPER
● **Trimming by hand** Some expensive wallpapers may not have perfectly straight edges. Trim them with sharp scissors before application.
● **Dealing with length** Most of the lengths you cut will be longer than the pasting board itself, so allow the wallpaper to concertina back on itself, taking care not to crease it.
● **Cutting** When you have marked off measurements on the wallpaper, use a ruler to draw a guideline. Cut across this line. You may soon be able to cut a straight line by eye.

MEASURING EASILY

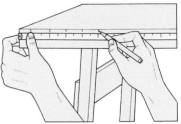

Marking a pasting table
Turn the edge of a pasting table into a ruler by marking off increments accurately and at appropriate intervals along the table's length. Measure lengths of wallpaper against this instead of using a ruler every time.

LINING WALLS

To improve wallpaper finish, it is worth lining the walls first: many manufacturers recommend it. The same techniques for wallpaper apply to lining paper, with a few minor adjustments.

● **Levelling** Lining paper does not have to be exactly vertical, since it is not seen. Treat each wall as a self-contained unit.
● **Sizing** Size lined surfaces once they are dry using a diluted paste solution mixed according to the manufacturer's guidelines. Sizing will allow you to move paper easily when positioning it.
● **Scaling edges** Seal trimmed edges with flexible filler to prevent them from lifting and to give a good edge against which you can trim wallpaper.

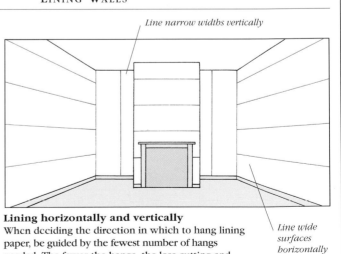

Line narrow widths vertically

Line wide surfaces horizontally

Lining horizontally and vertically
When deciding the direction in which to hang lining paper, be guided by the fewest number of hangs needed. The fewer the hangs, the less cutting and trimming. Horizontal lining around a chimney breast makes trimming and rounding the corners easier.

PASTING UP

Wallpaper requires adhesive to attach it to a wall. You can either mix wallpaper paste yourself or buy it pre-mixed and apply it to the wallpaper. Some wallpapers are ready-pasted – water activates a coating on the back – while others require that you apply paste to the wall.

MIXING PASTE
● **Stirring well** Stir paste for longer than suggested by the manufacturer to ensure that there are no lumps. A wooden dowel makes an ideal stirrer. Also stir the paste from time to time during wallpapering.

PASTING PAPER
● **Keeping paper flat** To stop wallpaper rolling up, weight each end before you start. Cover evenly with paste. Fold it into a loose, crease-free concertina as you move along from one end to the other.

KEEPING PAPER CLEAN
● **Protecting from paste** Paste each length in the same position – flush with the edge of the pasting table – to avoid getting paste on the right side. Wipe the table with clean, warm water between lengths.

DEALING WITH READY-PASTED WALLPAPER

MONEY-SAVING TIP

Using a kitchen table
Spread a plastic sheet over a kitchen table, and use it as a pasting table instead of buying one. Make sure that the sheet is held taut by taping it securely at each corner to the table legs.

Rolling up wallpaper
Ready-pasted wallpaper needs soaking to activate the paste. Loosely roll up a cut length with the pattern on the inside so that water will come into contact with all the pasted surface easily, thus activating the paste.

Folding soaked paper
Let soaked wallpaper unroll on a pasting table. Fold each end back on itself into the middle of the length so that the pattern is on the outside. This will prevent the pasted side from drying out before you apply it to the wall.

HANDLING DAMP PAPER
● **Protecting wallpaper** As you transfer wallpaper from the container in which it is being soaked to a pasting table, the patterned side of the wallpaper may rub on the side of the table and be damaged. Soften the edges of the table by covering them with two or three layers of masking tape.
● **Anchoring edges** Have a small pot of ready-mixed paste handy as you prepare to hang a length of wallpaper. The edges of ready-pasted wallpaper sometimes dry out too quickly, and you may need to apply a little more paste before you hang them.

STORING WALLPAPER WHILE IT SOAKS

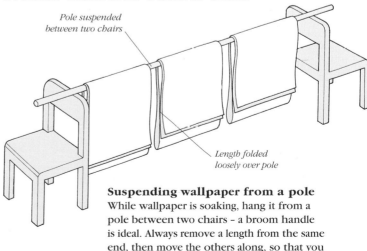

Pole suspended between two chairs

Length folded loosely over pole

Suspending wallpaper from a pole
While wallpaper is soaking, hang it from a pole between two chairs - a broom handle is ideal. Always remove a length from the same end, then move the others along, so that you take the one that has soaked longest.

HANGING WALLPAPER

However much preparation you do, a good hanging technique is vital to give a quality finish to your wallpapered walls. It is important to master the basic method of application so that when you come across obstacles, you will have a sound technique on which to build.

STARTING ACCURATELY

Finding the vertical
Use a spirit level as a straight edge to draw a pencil guideline at your chosen starting point on the wall. Extend this line by carefully moving the level down the wall to make sure of an accurate and continuous guide.

ADDRESSING A WALL

Preventing tears
Wallpaper that has been folded while soaking is more likely to tear, so support its weight with one hand as you unroll it. Make the first contact about 15 cm (6 in) below the ceiling, and follow guidelines down the wall.

HANGING SUCCESSFULLY
● **Allowing for expansion** When measuring out where lengths will hang, bear in mind that wallpaper expands from its dry measurement once it is pasted. Make an allowance of up to 0.5 cm ($\frac{1}{4}$ in).
● **Smoothing wallpaper** Brush from the centre of a length out towards and over the edges, and from top to bottom. This removes air bubbles.
● **Using embossed wallpaper** Do not apply too much pressure, otherwise the raised pattern will be flattened.
● **Applying vinyl** Take care not to stretch vinyl wallpaper while smoothing it. This can distort its edges and make it difficult to join to the next hang.

TRIMMING WALLPAPER

Making a precise dividing line between wallpaper and the adjacent surfaces is important for the production of a neat and well-defined finished product. Sharp scissors and craft knives, and a steady, accurate cutting technique are required to achieve this aim.

MONEY-SAVING TIP

Use an indelible felt-tip pen

Labelling craft-knife blades
Mark a dot on one end of a new craft-knife blade. Always use the marked end first, so that when you need to change the blade around you will be sure that the other end has not been used.

HIDING UNEVEN LINES

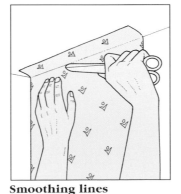

Smoothing lines
Where the wall–ceiling junction is not a straight edge, overlap the wallpaper slightly on to the ceiling, make a crease line with a pair of scissors, then trim. This will create a straighter line.

FIXING OVERTRIMMING

Hiding joins
If you have trimmed too much wallpaper, insert a small slither at the top behind the main length. Overlap the main length on to the slither. The overlap will not be seen from the ground.

JOINING WALLPAPER

Joining wallpaper accurately is as important as trimming well. You need to make neat, matching joins between lengths with no overlaps or gaps between hangs. Most wallpaper should meet exactly – in what is called a butt join – to give a smooth, perfectly matching finish.

MAKING PERFECT SEAMS

● **Underbrushing** Brush only enough to remove air bubbles and secure wallpaper firmly to the wall. Overbrushing tends to polish seams, which will shine once wallpaper is dry.

● **Using a seam roller** Run a seam roller lightly up and down a join to secure the wallpaper and make a join that is almost invisible. Do not use a seam roller on embossed wallpapers, since it will flatten the relief.

● **Repasting seams** Wallpaper edges are the first areas to lift over time, so stick them down well. After a few lengths have been hung, return to the first hangs and repaste any lifting edges using a fitch. Smooth with a damp sponge.

CENTRALIZING A WALLPAPER PATTERN

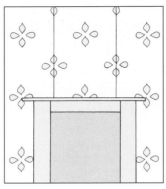 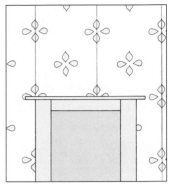

Centralized   Random

Using a feature within the room

Wallpaper with a medium- to large-sized pattern should always be centred on a focal point in a room (above left). This creates a well-balanced feel which sets off the rest of the decoration. Leaving where the pattern falls to chance might result in an off-centre look (above right), which would draw attention to the focal point for the wrong reason. Start wallpapering from the focal point (see p. 43).

KEEPING WALLPAPER CLEAN

Wallpaper is a delicate, and often expensive, decorating material, and you should look after it carefully so that the surface does not become spoiled. Always keep a supply of clean water to hand for any cleaning requirements throughout the entire decorating project.

SEGREGATING TOOLS

Colour co-ordinating

Keep different-coloured buckets and sponges for different tasks. This will prevent items used for cleaning the pasting table, which soon become dirty, from being confused with those for wallpaper.

REMOVING EXCESS PASTE

● **Cleaning adjacent surfaces** After wallpaper lengths have been trimmed, remove excess paste from the paper surface. In addition, clean the ceiling and skirting before any paste dries and dulls the surface.

● **Cutting new lengths** However often you wash down a pasting table, it may become tacky. To prevent wallpaper from becoming sticky while being cut, cover the table first with a sheet of lining paper.

● **Disposing of rubbish** As soon as each length is hung, immediately place offcuts in a bin bag. This will reduce the risk of paste being spread throughout the working area.

KEEPING YOUR WORK STATION CLEAN

It is advisable to keep surfaces and wallpapering equipment as clean as possible at all times to ensure the best results.

● **Removing excess paste** Scrape semi-dry paste off a pasting table using the blade of a scraper, especially around the edge of the table.

● **Replacing water** Fill the cleaning bucket with a fresh supply of water after about ten lengths have been pasted.

● **Drying equipment** Keep scissors and craft-knife blades dry at all times by wiping with lint-free cloth.

WALLPAPERING AWKWARD AREAS

WITHIN ANY ROOM you are likely to have to modify your basic wallpapering technique in order to deal with non-straightforward areas. Once learned, however, these adaptations will become part of your wallpapering repertoire.

AROUND WINDOWS AND DOORS

Windows and doors are commonplace obstacles in most rooms of the house, and you need to learn the correct procedure for negotiating them. Stick to a systematic approach that can be adapted depending on the design and size of each door and window.

COPING WITH OPENINGS

● **Sorting out damp** Window recesses may be affected by condensation in damp climates. To prevent wallpaper from lifting, run a bead of clear silicone all the way around the frame–paper junction to secure the wallpaper firmly.

● **Overlapping** Small overlaps may be unavoidable around a window. Try to position overlapping seams so that curtains will conceal them.

● **Preventing accidents** Lock a door when wallpapering above it to prevent it from opening while you are on a ladder. If the door does not lock, pin a warning note to the other side, or put an obstacle there.

WALLPAPERING ACCORDING TO PLAN

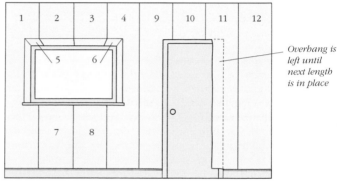

Overhang is left until next length is in place

Following a logical sequence
Wallpaper a wall that includes windows and doors in a certain order (1–12) to maintain the vertical as you wallpaper around them. Hang 12 before you trim 11 to ensure that 12 is vertical. If you trimmed 11 first, and followed that line, 12 might not be completely vertical.

WALLPAPERING ARCHWAYS

Overlaps are inevitable in archways, since wallpaper cannot stretch in different directions around a corner. This need not be a problem as long as overlaps are made correctly.

● **Choosing wallpaper** When joining wallpapers between rooms, use the one with the smallest design in the archway to minimize the pattern break.

● **Avoiding wallpapering** Wallpaper to the edge of an archway, but paint the inside the same colour as the ceiling in the adjacent room. This will link the archway with that room and avoid wallpapering.

Moulding wallpaper
Make small, right-angled cuts in the wallpaper. It will then fold easily into an archway. You will cover the cuts with the length of wallpaper that you apply to the inside of the archway.

WALLPAPERING AROUND FITTINGS

Consider carefully whether or not you will want to move fittings and pictures around once you have decorated.

● **Removing picture hooks** Remove all hooks before you decorate. You may decide once you have finished that you would like to reposition pictures or mirrors.

● **Marking shelving** If shelves or other fittings are to stay in the same position, take them down and reinsert the fixings. When you wallpaper, they will poke through, revealing themselves for refitting.

AROUND CORNERS

Occasionally wallpaper will bend around corners easily. When corners are not square or even, however, you will have to adjust your wallpapering technique when continuing the paper on to the adjacent wall. Check again that the hang is vertical as you start a new wall.

WALLPAPERING SUCCESSFULLY AROUND UNEVEN EXTERNAL CORNERS

1 Extend a length of wallpaper around an external corner. Hang the next length so that it overlaps the previous one by 5–10 cm (2–4 in). Cut through the centre of the overlap.

2 Carefully peel back the edges of the overlap, and remove the two strips of excess wallpaper. Support the wallpaper with one hand to avoid any possibility of tearing.

3 Smooth the seam with a wallpaper-hanging brush to form a perfect butt join. Before the paste dries, remove any excess from around the join with a damp sponge.

WALLPAPERING SUCCESSFULLY AROUND UNEVEN INTERNAL CORNERS

● **Joining in corners** Wallpaper around an internal corner and trim 2.5 cm (1 in) beyond. Place the next length on the second wall over the strip.

● **Cornering easily** To fit paper around an internal corner, cut two small slits at both the top and bottom of the length at the ceiling and skirting board.

● **Preventing lifting** To ensure that wallpaper will not lift, run border adhesive along the entire overlap with a fitch. This is essential with vinyl papers.

WALLPAPERING STAIRWELLS

Wallpapering a stairwell involves handling long lengths, angled trimming, and rounding corners.

● **Sharing the job** It is easier for two people to handle long lengths of wallpaper. One can position the top of a length while the other supports it.

● **Measuring hangs** Measuring is difficult because the bottom edge of each hang is angled. Start at the bottom of the stairs, and work up. This will make angled cutting easier to perform.

● **Pasting and soaking** Paste only one length at a time. Keep soaking times consistent so that all lengths expand equally and patterns will match up exactly.

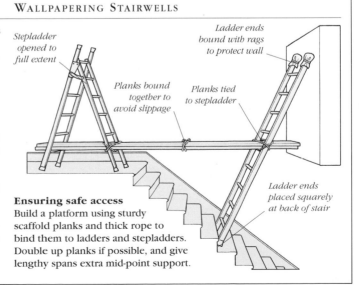

Stepladder opened to full extent

Ladder ends bound with rags to protect wall

Planks bound together to avoid slippage

Planks tied to stepladder

Ladder ends placed squarely at back of stair

Ensuring safe access
Build a platform using sturdy scaffold planks and thick rope to bind them to ladders and stepladders. Double up planks if possible, and give lengthy spans extra mid-point support.

AROUND ELECTRICAL FITTINGS

Electrical fittings are like any other obstacles you might come across when wallpapering, and they need not present a problem as long as you follow the correct procedures. Take care to observe the necessary safety precautions when wallpapering around electrical fittings.

PREPARING ELECTRICS

● **Doing electrical work** If you have a room rewired, ask the electrician not to fit switch socket plates and wall fittings until the wallpapering is finished. Use portable lights from another room temporarily.

● **Coping with wall lights** Plan wallpapering so that seams will occur behind the centre of a light fitting. You will then need only to loosen the fitting and slip the wallpaper behind.

WARNING!
Before wallpapering around electrical fittings, turn off the power. Wallpaper paste is a good conductor, so do not allow it near exposed wires.

WALLPAPERING AROUND AN ELECTRICAL SWITCH

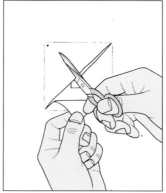

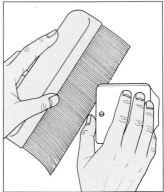

1 Paper loosely over a switch. Make a pencil mark just in from each corner impression in the wallpaper. Cut from the centre out to each mark. Trim the resulting triangular flaps to leave a square hole.

2 Loosen the switch screws. Ease the plate away from the wall and in front of the wallpaper. Using a wallpaper-hanging brush, smooth the paper behind the plate. Replace screws, and wipe the plate clean.

AROUND PIPES AND RADIATORS

Pipes and radiators are awkward obstacles around which to wallpaper. They have no straight edges to trim against, and it may be necessary to wallpaper the wall behind them. These obstacles can be overcome with a few adjustments to basic wallpapering techniques.

COPING WITH RADIATORS

Papering behind a radiator
If a radiator is bracketed to the wall, allow wallpaper to fall over it. Cut slits in line with the brackets. Using a radiator roller, feed the wallpaper behind, guiding it around the brackets.

AVOIDING PROBLEMS

● **Starting with pipes** Start your wallpapering behind a pipe so that the joining seam will be hidden by it. By doing this you will also eliminate the need for complicated trimming around the pipe brackets.

● **Keeping pipes clean** Remove wallpaper paste from bare metal pipes immediately, since it can cause corrosion, which in turn results in the unsightly staining of the pipes.

● **Removing obstacles** Hire a professional plumber to remove radiators and cap off the pipes before you start to wallpaper. This is a quick, inexpensive job that will make wallpapering much easier.

BRIGHT IDEA

Wallpapering behind pipes
Unscrew and remove pipe brackets, and feed wallpaper behind the pipes. Replace the brackets while you can locate the screw holes easily through the wet wallpaper.

ADDING BORDERS

Borders are an important wallpapering accessory: they complement or highlight features of the wallpaper. Many borders are designed for use with a particular wallpaper, but they can also be used against a plain coloured wall.

ATTACHING BORDERS

Apply a border once the rest of the wall decoration has been completed. Whether the border is narrow or broad, textured or plain, the application method is the same. Attach a border very carefully in order to enhance the appearance of the already decorated wall.

POSITIONING BORDERS

● **Planning position** You can hang borders at ceiling, dado-rail, picture-rail, or skirting-board level. Consider uneven wall–ceiling junctions, split-level ceilings, and the location of switches and other obstacles when making your decision.
● **Keeping level** If placing a border on wallpaper, follow a horizontal line in the pattern. If this is impossible, draw a guideline using a spirit level.
● **Pasting up** Apply adhesive to a border with a small brush and place it on the wall right away. Border adhesive dries quickly, so do not soak it unless the instructions say so.

CREATING DADOS

Using a border
Use a wallpaper border instead of a wooden or plaster dado rail to divide up an expanse of wall. This will be decorative without the fixing requirements and cost.

CHOOSING APPROPRIATELY

Co-ordinating details
Choose a border with an image that suits the room as well as matching the decor. In a child's bedroom, for example, pick a simple, brightly coloured motif.

FRAMING WITH BORDERS

Mitring a corner
Allow one length of border to overlap the other with the pattern corresponding. Cut diagonally through both with a craft knife. Remove excess flaps, and smooth the remaining pieces into place.

APPLYING BORDERS

● **Cornering** Apply one length of border so that it overlaps on to the adjacent wall by 0.5 cm ($\frac{1}{8}$ in). Overlap the next length on to it so that the pattern matches at the join. Crease down the corner junction with a pair of scissors, and pull back the paper. Cut accurately down the crease guideline. Smooth the border back into place, producing a matching join in the corner with an invisible overlap.
● **Hanging quickly** Use a damp sponge rather than a wallpaper-hanging brush to position a border and remove any excess border adhesive quickly before it dries.

MONEY-SAVING TIP

Making your own border
Trim an old, leftover roll of wallpaper to create your own border. Wallpaper with a striped pattern is ideal since it provides a ready-made guideline along which to cut.

CHOOSING OTHER WALL COVERINGS

T HERE ARE MANY OPTIONS other than wallpaper for wall decoration. They include highly textured papers, different types of fabric, and the use of wood, wooden panelling, and plaster if you prefer a heavy decorative finish.

WALL HANGINGS

I n its most traditional form, a wall hanging consists of decorative fabric that is hung on a wall in a similar way to pictures and paintings.

However, wall-hanging options do not stop there, since there are other ways of attaching decorative materials to a flat wall surface.

CHOOSING TEXTURED WALL COVERINGS

Some wall coverings fix to a wall like wallpaper but have a genuine fabric texture. Many less traditional wall coverings are proprietary products that require specific hanging systems.

● Selecting fabrics for texture
Choose silk if you want to produce a very sumptuous finish. Hessian and grasscloth are much coarser in texture and create a rustic, earthy feel.
● Choosing unusual textures
Modern ranges of wall coverings include some unusual options. You might like to create the impression on your wall of a hewn rock face or fine mineral particles like sand or stones.

Silk

Hessian

Grasscloth

Stone effect

HANGING UNUSUAL ITEMS

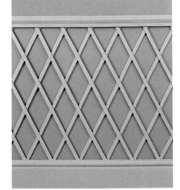

Using a garden trellis
Hang a simple, painted garden trellis beneath a dado rail for an unusual decoration. A trellis is light, so you can attach it with any wood-fixing compound.

HANGING RUGS & CARPETS SUCCESSFULLY

● **Hanging flush** To attach a rug to a wall, screw a length of carpet gripper rod to the wall where the top of the rug will be placed. Press the rug firmly on to the rod's teeth.

● **Using curtain poles** If a rug or carpet has a looped fringe, thread the loops along a curtain pole. Attach this to the wall with the appropriate brackets supplied with it.

Featuring rugs
Rugs and other wall hangings come in all shapes and sizes, so you should be able to find ones to fit in with your decorative ideas. Choose unusual shapes, and place them in less obvious positions such as above a window to create a point of special interest.

ATTACHING FABRICS

● **Using battens** Screw in battens at ceiling and skirting level. Use a staple gun to attach a piece of fabric (that has been cut to size) to the battens. Staple the material along the top batten, then stretch it down to the bottom batten, and fix it to that. For more texture, pleat the fabric as you staple it.
● **Covering staples** Hide the staple heads fixing the material by placing a strip of fabric over the battens using fabric glue.
● **Cleaning easily** Attach lightweight fabric using touch-and-close tape. The fabric can then be taken down and washed whenever necessary.

WOOD PANELLING

Walls can be covered completely or in part with wooden panels to create a substantial decorative impact. Paint them or leave them natural, depending on your preference. You will need one or two woodworking tools and a few basic carpentry skills to panel successfully.

PANELLING CLEVERLY
● **Allowing access** Cut access pieces into wood panelling in order to reach pipework and to house electrical sockets.
● **Covering edges** Neaten cuts and joins in panelling at ceiling level by attaching lengths of decorative wooden moulding using panel pins.
● **Faking wood panels** To create the effect of wooden panels on a wall, cut four equal-sized lengths of moulding or architrave, mitring the ends to make the corners of the panels. Place each piece in position on the wall, using an all-purpose adhesive. A number of such panels beneath a dado, for example, creates a realistic effect – especially if the panels are grained (see p. 79).

BUILDING A FRAMEWORK
● **Using battens** Attach panels to a framework made of 5-cm by 2.5-cm (2-in by 1-in) battens placed horizontally on the wall, about 30 cm (12 in) apart.

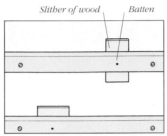
Slither of wood   *Batten*

Infilling gaps
If a wall is not absolutely flat, pack out gaps behind the battens of the framework so that they are flush with the wall. Wedge slithers of wood behind the battens before securing them.

ATTACHING PANELLING
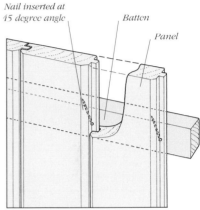
Nail inserted at 15 degree angle   *Batten*   *Panel*

Hiding fixings
When attaching tongue-and-groove panelling, insert a nail through the tongue of one length into the batten behind it. The groove of the adjacent panel will hide it when put in place.

DECORATIVE MOULDINGS

Decorative mouldings create an impression of detail and are generally used to add a finishing touch to wall decoration. Mouldings can be made of wood, plaster, or polystyrene and are produced in ever-increasing variety. Standard coving is still the most popular choice.

REPAIRING COVING
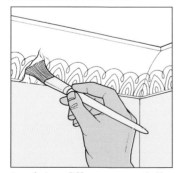

Applying filler successfully
It can be difficult to apply filler to ornate coving that has been damaged or has cracked. Use your finger to put the filler in place, then mould it into shape and smooth it with a damp fitch.

FIXING PLASTER COVING
● **Starting with the finish** Although coving is in effect a finishing, it should be applied before the decorating process begins. Fill and paint it before the walls are decorated.
● **Attaching** Use nails and adhesive to attach coving, since it needs support while the adhesive dries. Manufacturers suggest that nails can then be removed, but they are best left, filled, and painted over.
● **Smoothing** It is difficult to sand moulding adhesive when dry, so remove rough areas and smooth joints while wet. After each piece has been applied, smooth with a damp sponge.

CHOOSING POLYSTYRENE COVING

Although less solid and realistic in appearance than plaster, polystyrene coving is much less expensive than its plaster equivalents.

● **Flexible** Because it is more flexible, polystyrene coving is easier to position, more suitable for uneven wall–ceiling junctions, and less likely to suffer from cracks.
● **Easy to use** Polystyrene is lightweight and easy to work with. To give it a more solid look, apply several coats of paint to fill the small holes that characterize its make-up.

FINISHING OFF

I T IS IMPORTANT TO TAKE TIME to complete your wallpapering properly so that the finish looks as good as it possibly can, and will last a long time. Make future decorating projects easier by looking after your equipment very carefully.

CORRECTING MISTAKES

S ome problems may develop after you have finished wallpapering. Most of these will be fairly minor and easily put right, although they will need attending to. Problems arising from serious deficiencies in technique may need more extensive work in order to correct them.

REMOVING STAINS

● **Dealing with damp patches**
Damp patches that persist after wallpaper has dried out may indicate a structural problem. Strip the paper off and line the whole area with proprietary damp-resistant foil before wallpapering again.
● **Using detergent** Remove miscellaneous stains and marks with a mild household detergent solution, dabbed on and wiped off with a sponge. Rub extremely gently.

IMPROVING MATCHING

● **Distracting the eye** Use a picture or wall hanging to detract from a mismatch. Always rectify or conceal any that occur at eye level.
● **Repapering** Apply another layer of paper to cover a bad pattern mismatch but only in small-scale, localized areas.

EVENING OFF EDGES

● **Sticking down** In bathrooms and kitchens, paper can lift at tiled edges because of excess moisture and poor adhesion. Run a thin band of grout or sealant over the paper at the tile–paper junction. Use masking tape to ensure a straight line.
● **Painting** If paper is poorly trimmed and overlaps on to wood, it will look bad and may lift. If necessary, paint over any overlapping paper using the woodwork paint.

RECTIFYING WALLPAPERING FAULTS

There are several fairly common wallpapering faults that may well affect only small areas, yet can spoil your decorating if they are not corrected. However good your technique, faults can occur, but most can be solved using a few relatively simple methods.

Gaping seams
Use a felt-tip pen that matches the background colour of the wallpaper to colour in seams that have not been joined properly, or which have opened slightly as the wallpaper dried. Remove excess colour by dabbing with a clean, damp sponge.

Shiny seams
Wipe down shiny or stained seams with a mild detergent solution to make them less conspicuous. To prevent shine when wallpapering in the future, remove any excess wallpaper paste from seams before it dries, and do not oversmooth seams.

Lifting edges
Stick back lifting edges with overlap adhesive or neat PVA. Use a fitch to apply the adhesive along the entire length of the area that is lifting. Wipe away excess adhesive that spills out from beneath the edge with a clean, damp sponge.

Paper tears
Apply a small amount of neat PVA to the surface, and ease the torn piece of wallpaper back into position using a clean, damp sponge. As long as you manoeuvre the wallpaper carefully back into place, the repair will be almost invisible.

Bubbling
Most bubbles should disappear of their own accord as the wallpaper dries out. If they do not, pierce them with a sharp craft knife, and stick the area back down with neat PVA. Apply it very carefully with a fitch or a small artist's brush.

CLEANING AND MAINTAINING EQUIPMENT

After all types of decorating work – and wallpapering is no exception – make sure that you clean your equipment well, so that it will be in good working order in future. Many tools are costly to replace, and it is all too easy to ruin them through needless neglect.

CLEANING SURFACES
● **Using soap** Wash down a pasting table with mild detergent after use, otherwise any paste residue might be reactivated by water the next time the table is used.

CARING FOR BRUSHES
● **Softening bristles** Clean wallpapering brushes with a mild shampoo, then rinse them thoroughly. This will ensure that they remain soft until the next time they are used.

STORING SPIRIT LEVELS
● **Hanging up** Most spirit levels have a hook on one end for hanging up after use. They are delicate and should be kept out of harm's way. Clean any paste off them first.

PROTECTING SCISSORS

Oiling a hinge
Use a lint-free cloth to apply oil to the hinging mechanism once scissors have been washed and dried. Do not use too much oil, or it may stain the paper next time.

MAINTAINING WALLPAPERED WALLS

There are several different ways to maintain and thus prolong the life of wall coverings.

● **Following recommendations** Check the label to see if you can wipe or scrub wallpaper.
● **Protecting paper** Apply a protective coat of acrylic matt varnish. Do a test patch in case the varnish reacts with the paper.
● **Caring for fabrics** Use a soft vacuum-cleaner attachment to remove dust from fabric-based, textured wall coverings.

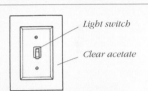

Light switch

Clear acetate

Making cleaning easy
Fit a rectangular-shaped piece of acetate (with a central area the size of the switch cut out of it) around an electrical switch. The wallpaper will still be visible, but you will be able to keep this frequently soiled area clean.

USING LEFTOVERS

Applying a wall covering tends to be a rather wasteful business, so try to use up some of the leftover pieces. Wallpaper pieces can be used for a variety of different purposes. Always keep some in case you have to make patch repairs to a wallpapered surface in future.

USING UP WALLPAPER
● **Wrapping gifts** Cut up offcuts of patterned wallpaper for wrapping up presents.
● **Enhancing decoration** Cover the panels of cupboard doors with wallpaper to add an extra decorative dimension to your papering. This will help to co-ordinate the decorative scheme as well as enhancing a plain piece of furniture.
● **Using pattern** Patterns that include distinctive motifs can be cut up, and the motifs put to use for a variety of other decorative purposes such as *découpage* (see p. 85) or making a stencil (see p. 35).

MAXIMIZING USE
● **Recycling blades** Craft-knife blades are still relatively sharp even after they have been used for trimming wallpaper. Since only the tip of the blade will have been used, you can continue to use the blade for other purposes such as cutting carpet prior to fitting it.
● **Keeping paste** If there is a chance that you may do more wallpapering shortly after your current project, do not throw away leftover wallpaper paste. It can be kept for several weeks, or even a few months, as long as you can transfer it to an airtight container.

MONEY-SAVING TIP

Lining a drawer
Trim wallpaper offcuts to use as drawer liners. Iron and spray-starch each length so that it will sit flat inside a drawer. Secure in place with drawing pins if necessary.

TILING WALLS

*A*S WELL AS BEING *highly decorative, tiles are a practical material for use in home decoration. They provide a hardwearing surface that is long-lasting and easy to clean. Many home decorators are reluctant to face tiling challenges, and defer to experts. But cutting equipment, tile adhesives, and grout are more user-friendly than they used to be, so tiling is not as difficult as you might think.*

SETTING A STYLE

The vast range of wall tiles available gives you ample opportunity to make creative decisions about the style, design, and layout of a tiled area. Choosing a style and creating your own tile designs are easy as long as you take a few basics into account before you start out.

BUDGETING WISELY
● **Planning** Tiles vary widely in price, so always bear your budget in mind. Less expensive tiles need not mean a less attractive finish.

APPRAISING YOUR SKILLS
● **Being realistic** Tile within your capabilities. If you are a first-time tiler, choose a simple project to start with. Proficiency will come with experience.

SAMPLING TILES
● **Borrowing tiles** If you find it difficult to visualize what tiles will look like, borrow some samples from a supplier to take home and try out "dry".

ARRANGING WALL TILES

When you are choosing a design for the layout of an area to be tiled, you may find yourself limited by the size of the area. Bear in mind its practical purpose, and take the following stylistic points into account.

● **Choosing a basic style** The first aspect to consider when arranging wall tiles is whether to follow a traditional style of tiling, or choose from the range of modern styles, or adopt a more individualistic approach.
● **Thinking about colour** When deciding which kind of design to create, consider the colour of the tiles. Think in terms of the decoration of the whole room as well as colour combinations within the tiled area itself.

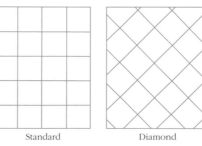

Standard   Diamond   Inset border

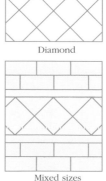 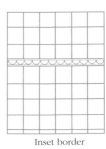 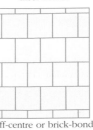

Edged border   Mixed sizes   Off-centre or brick-bond

CHOOSING TILES

Size and shape are as important as colour when you are choosing tiles. However much you like a particular tile, you must consider where it is going to be used. It is not advisable, for example, to choose a complicated design or large tiles if the area to be tiled is small.

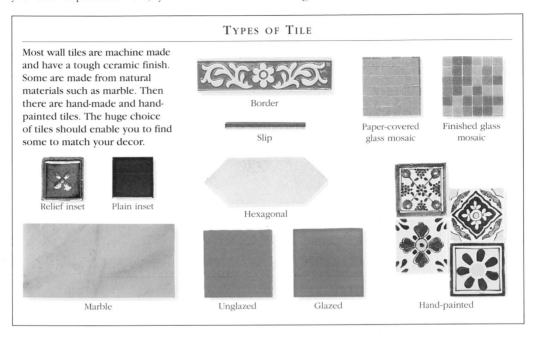

TYPES OF TILE

Most wall tiles are machine made and have a tough ceramic finish. Some are made from natural materials such as marble. Then there are hand-made and hand-painted tiles. The huge choice of tiles should enable you to find some to match your decor.

Border

Slip

Paper-covered glass mosaic

Finished glass mosaic

Relief inset

Plain inset

Hexagonal

Marble

Unglazed

Glazed

Hand-painted

CO-ORDINATING TILES WITH DECOR

Tiles have little impact unless they are well co-ordinated with the rest of the decor in a room. Extravagant tile designs require the rest of the decoration to be complementary, while a less complex design allows other decorative features to make a greater statement.

CONSIDERING OPTIONS
● **Choosing colours** Stick to plain, neutral colours for your tiles if you are concerned about changing styles and fashions. Remember that you will find it much easier to redecorate around neutral-coloured tiles than around bold colours and designs that make a strong statement.
● **Using picture tiles** The most common way of adding more interest to a plain tiled surface is to include some picture tiles. However, be cautious in your choice: too many picture tiles can make a design look overdone, detracting from the rest of the tiled surface and from the room as a whole.

INTRODUCING THEMES
● **Adding interest** Incorporate a few themed tiles into a plain tiled design to transform the appearance of a tiled surface.

Using relief tiles
Include relief tiles in a tiled area to add another dimension. Here, a few frogs leaping along a tiled splashback tie in with the theme of running water in a bathroom.

CO-ORDINATING COLOUR

Using colour boldly
Use a tiled area to make a bold colour statement. Paint a piece of furniture so that it picks up one of the colours in the tiles, thus co-ordinating the decor.

PREPARING TO TILE

T ILED AREAS TEND TO BE REDECORATED INFREQUENTLY because tiles are expensive and more of a permanent fixture than other wall coverings. You are likely to live with them for a while, so prepare well and do a thorough job.

BASIC TILING EQUIPMENT

A toolkit for tiling will include a few more specialist tools than are required for most other decorating jobs. However, some general tools are, in effect, multi-purpose and lend themselves to a number of different tasks.

● **Choosing a tile cutter** By far the most important piece of equipment you will buy for tiling purposes is a tile cutter. Buy a good-quality one, since a sub-standard cutter will not produce clean edges and will increase the number of tiles that you break while cutting. This is wasteful of materials and time, and will result in greater expense in the long run.
● **Buying wisely** Do not be deterred by the initial expense of a few key tiling items: they may prove themselves to be worth it in the long term, especially as your technique improves.
● **Hiring instead of buying** Consider hiring expensive pieces of equipment such as tile-cutting machines, which you will use only occasionally.

Power drill

Tile file

Score-and-snap pliers

Tile scorer

Tile saw

Nibbler

Sponge

Tile spacers

Tile cutter

Sealant dispenser

Pointing trowel

Felt-tip pen

Tape measure

Filling knife

Spirit level

Notched spreader

Grout spreader

Goggles

Tile gauge

MAKING SURFACES READY

It is essential that tiles make good contact with a wall by means of a consistent and even spread of adhesive. Walls do not have to be perfectly smooth, as long as the surface is sealed, is as flat as possible, and has no unstable areas that may cause tiles to bulge or fall away.

PREPARING A WALL

● **Filling** Fill major holes with all-purpose filler. Before it dries, trim rough areas with a filling knife so that no pieces protrude. These patches will not be smooth, but are quite adequate for tiles. You do not need to sand the walls.

● **Removing old coverings** Do not tile over paper, however firmly attached it may appear to be. The adhesive and weight of the new tiles will almost certainly pull it away.

● **Sealing** Stabilize dusty walls or new plaster with a PVA solution (five parts water to one PVA) before tiling.

DEALING WITH OBSTACLES

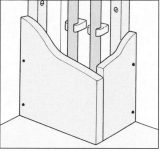

Boxing in

Create a neat, flat surface around obstacles such as pipes by boxing them in. Use a simple, battened framework covered with MDF, which should be thick enough not to bow when it is tiled.

TILING OVER TILES

Old tiles make an excellent base for new as long as they are securely stuck to the wall.

● **Replacing damaged tiles** Remove cracked tiles, and fill the areas with one-coat plaster. This will be more economical than filler, especially if you have to remove several tiles.

● **Avoiding joints** Make sure that new tiles join in different places from those beneath.

● **Providing a key** Wash down old tiles with sugar soap, allow to dry, then sand with fine-grade sandpaper to provide a key for the new layer of tiles.

MEASURING UP

Accuracy when measuring is important so that over-calculations, which can prove expensive, and inconvenient under-calculations are avoided. You must first decide how much of a room to tile. Small variations at a later stage will make a large difference to requirements.

MAKING ALLOWANCES

● **Allowing for pictures** Picture tiles are usually more expensive than plain tiles, so you should calculate exactly how many you need, rather than working out the size of the area.

● **Tiling borders** Measure the total length of border tiles required rather than their area. Remember, however, to deduct the border area when you are calculating the area of the main body of tiles.

● **Using tiles of different sizes** If you wish to incorporate a complicated design in your tiled area, including tiles of different sizes for example, ask a tile retailer to work out your precise requirements. Supply a drawing of the tile design and the measurements of the area to be tiled.

MAKING A TILE GAUGE

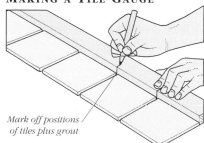

Mark off positions of tiles plus grout

Using a batten

Mark off tile-width measurements along a batten, either using sample tiles or based on tile sizes. Allow 2.5 mm (1/8 in) for grout between each tile. Use the gauge to calculate quantities of tiles and work out where cuts and joins will be.

CALCULATING QUANTITIES

Never estimate even the smallest part of a tiling area. Measure each section separately and accurately, then add the figures up to give the total area.

● **Measuring appropriately** Most retailers sell tiles in square metres (square yards), so work out coverage with this in mind.

● **Allowing for cuts and breaks** Add ten per cent to the figure you have calculated to allow for wastage from cutting and the occasional breakage. Increase this percentage for awkward-shaped rooms that have many corners and cuts, and reduce it slightly for rooms that have broad expanses of wall surface.

PLANNING A TILING STRATEGY

Tiles are rigid and inflexible, so it is not possible to disguise mistakes like you can with wallpaper. You must, therefore, calculate exactly where rows of tiles will be, plan awkward areas carefully, and determine where cuts will occur.

ORDERING WORK

Tiling different sections in the correct order speeds up the job and produces the best finish. Take a little extra time to decide how you are going to tackle a particular area, and to ensure that all equipment and materials are close to hand, clean, and ready for use.

STARTING OUT

● **Mixing tiles** When tiling a large area, mix up different boxes of tiles in case there are colour variations between batches. You will not see them when the tiles are on the wall.

● **Starting at the bottom** Tile from the base of an area up.

● **Using natural levels** If baths, sinks, or skirting boards provide a natural base line within your tiling plan, use them as a starting point.

● **Accounting for corners** Make sure that corners look as if whole tiles are wrapped around them. Two small strips or two large offcuts meeting at a corner join look unattractive. If you cannot plan so that whole tiles meet in a corner, two half-tiles look best.

TILING A WALL SECTION BY SECTION

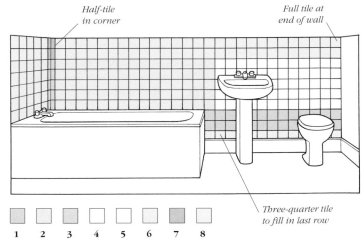

Half-tile in corner

Full tile at end of wall

Three-quarter tile to fill in last row

| 1 | 2 | 3 | 4 | 5 | 6 | 7 | 8 |

Dividing up a tiling area into sections
Tile sections according to a plan (1–8). Do the easiest parts of any one section first, leaving cuts and other intricacies until last. Plan so that whole tiles follow natural lines, such as the rim of a bath. Avoid using narrow slithers, and always check that tiles are level.

USING A TILE GAUGE

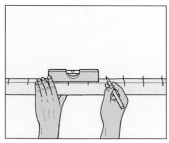

Measuring an area
Use a pencil and a tile gauge to mark all along the wall where the tiles should be placed. Make sure that the tile gauge remains horizontal by resting a small spirit level on its upper edge.

FOLLOWING GUIDELINES

● **Using non-square tiles** You will need a second tile gauge for rectangular or non-square tiles in order to produce accurate vertical guidelines.

● **Limiting height** Tile tall walls in 1-m (1-yd) sections at a time, otherwise the weight of the top layers can cause lower layers to bulge or pull away.

● **Checking tiles are flush** Use a tile gauge to see if tiles are flush to the wall. Run the flat edge across the tiled surface: it will knock against proud tiles, and show daylight in front of those that need building out.

MAKING A LEVEL BASE

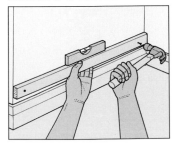

Attaching a batten
If there is no level base, carefully tack a batten to the wall, making sure that it is level, to create a base for tiling. When you have finished, remove the batten and fill in the area with cut tiles.

IMPROVING TECHNIQUES

ONCE YOU HAVE A TILING STRATEGY, the technique itself comes down to the mechanical process of applying adhesive and sticking tiles to a wall. Technical refinements include methods of cutting and applying adhesive.

CUTTING AND ATTACHING TILES

You will produce a flat and even tiled finish if you apply adhesive correctly, and if you take the right precautions to keep tiles level, both horizontally and vertically. Tiles cannot bend or stretch, so when you cut them make the incisions as precise as you possibly can.

APPLYING ADHESIVE

Using a notched spreader
Use a professional spreader to apply adhesive to a wall. Work in areas of up to 1 m² (1 sq yd), and make sure that the adhesive has a uniform, ridged appearance before applying any tiles.

LEVELLING TILED WALLS

Reducing adhesive
On uneven walls, vary the depth of adhesive for an even finish. Before the adhesive dries, lever out proud tiles using a wide-bladed scraper. Remove some of the adhesive, and replace the tile.

TRADITIONAL TIP

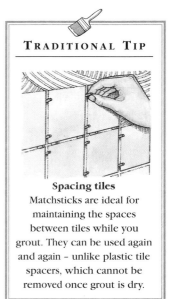

Spacing tiles
Matchsticks are ideal for maintaining the spaces between tiles while you grout. They can be used again and again – unlike plastic tile spacers, which cannot be removed once grout is dry.

TILING AROUND PLASTIC BATHS

Plastic fittings are prone to movement because they are flexible, so take extra care to ensure a good tiled finish.

● **Supporting** Provide extra support beneath a plastic bath to stop downward movement cracking the grout around the bottom row of tiles.
● **Filling** Fill a plastic bath with water before you start tiling around it so that it will be in the correct position and shape.
● **Sealing** Run silicone beading around the top of a plastic bath before tiling to make a barrier against water seepage.

PRE-EMPTING PROBLEMS

● **Using thin tiles** Spacers are too deep to be left in place between thin tiles, and may show through the grout. Use them at right angles to the joins, and remove before grouting.
● **Making allowances** When measuring tiles for cutting, allow 2.5 mm (⅛ in) for grout.
● **Tiling with marble** Marble tiles should give the appearance of a solid sheet, though grout is required for waterproofing. Use strips of thin card as spacers.
● **Reducing cleaning-up** Keep a damp sponge and a dry cloth handy so that you can keep tiles and hands clean at all times while you work.

CUTTING QUICKLY

Grip lever firmly

Tile cutter

Tile

Mounting a tile cutter
Using a tile cutter is the easiest way of making neat, accurate cuts. Mount the cutter on a workbench or clamp it to a table top to hold it firm and at the correct working height.

TILING AWKWARD AREAS

As with all decorating techniques, some areas are more difficult to tile than others. Corners, as you might expect, can present a challenge if you want them to look as neat as possible, and you may well have to cut intricate shapes to tile successfully around obstacles.

OVERCOMING OBSTACLES

● **Using a nibbler** To cut away awkward pieces of tile, use a nibbler. This resembles a pair of pliers, and enables you to chip off small sections of tile between the sharp-edged jaws.

● **Dealing with pipes** Remove any pipe brackets so that tiles can be slipped directly behind. Reposition brackets after tiling by drilling new holes in the tiles (see p. 70). Take care not to overtighten the screws, which might crack the tiles.

● **Tiling recesses** To provide support once downward-facing tiles have been attached along the top surface of a recessed window, cut three pieces of batten – one the width of the recess and two the height of it. Rest the two uprights on the windowsill, supporting the horizontal flush to the top tiles until the adhesive has dried.

TILING AROUND CURVED OBSTACLES

● **Measuring curves** Mould a pipe cleaner or flexible ruler to the shape of a curve, then draw along it on the tile to be cut.

● **Choosing a blade** Select a tungsten carbide blade to make a precise cut, and thus create the most accurate curve.

CUTTING CURVES USING A TEMPLATE

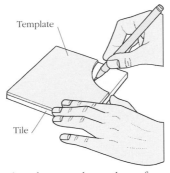

Template

Tile

Tile saw

1 Make a card template of a curve – allowing for the grout – and lay it on top of the tile. Trace around the edge with a non-permanent felt-tip pen, so that the ink guideline can be wiped off the tile later.

2 Use a specialist tile saw to cut around the shape of the curve accurately. Place the tile on a workbench, hold it very firmly, and cut – using a normal sawing action – along the guideline you have marked.

TILING EXTERNAL & INTERNAL CORNERS

Hiding edges

Attach a plastic corner strip to an external corner to conceal and protect tile edges. Fix the strip on to the corner with tile adhesive. Using whole tiles, tile away from the strip on each wall, aligning the tiles vertically with it.

Making a neat edge

When tiling an internal corner, place tiles alternately on each wall to ensure an even corner join and to keep the tiles level and in position. Leave gaps for grout in between the corner tiles using spacers in the usual way.

DEALING WITH SOCKETS AND SWITCHES

Tiling around sockets and switches offers no particular problems as long as you follow basic guidelines.

● **Turning off power** Always turn off the electricity supply before you begin work.

● **Loosening screws** Loosen electrical socket or switch screws so that tile edges can be inserted behind the socket plate. Do not retighten the screws until after grouting.

● **Adjusting screw length** If using thick tiles, it may be necessary to replace existing socket screws with longer ones, so that the socket plate can be screwed firmly back on to the electrical housing.

TILING CREATIVELY

Tiling is a flexible option when it comes to making decorative decisions. You can create a variety of designs and tile arrangements using different shapes and sizes of tile to lend an individualistic and personal look to any room.

CHOOSING TILES OF DIFFERENT SIZES

The most obvious alternative to traditional tiling methods is to use different-sized tiles to achieve various effects. Application methods are similar to standard tiling techniques. Minor refinements, however, can speed up the tiling process as well as improve the finish.

USING LARGE TILES
● **Choosing surfaces** Large tiles look most impressive on large wall surfaces rather than in small, detailed places. Too many half-tiles and joins detract from the overall look.
● **Using marble tiles** Use marble tiles only on dead flat wall surfaces, as undulations highlight grouted joins and spoil the "sheet" marble finish.
● **Cutting marble tiles** Cut marble tiles with a tile-cutting machine for greater accuracy. Ask your tile retailer to mitre external corner joins, or hire a table-top-mounted tile saw.

APPLYING MOSAICS

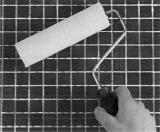

Bedding in
Use a short-pile roller to bed sheets of mosaic tiles into tile adhesive. This will ensure that you apply even pressure all over the area, so that the tiles stick firmly and lie flush to the wall.

USING SMALL TILES
● **Positioning tiles** Mosaic tiles within a sheet may drift out of position if the backing is defective. While the adhesive is still wet, reposition the tiles using the edge of a scraper, and support them with spacers.
● **Cutting tiles out** If the sheet backing will not allow you to reposition easily, cut the tile out of the sheet with a craft knife. Apply adhesive to the back and put it back in place, using spacers to keep it level.
● **Finishing edges** Cut up some of the mosaic sheets and use to edge other tiled areas.

DESIGNING LAYOUTS

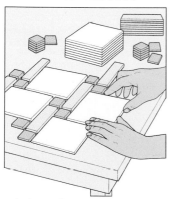

Mixing tile sizes
Lay out your tile design "dry" on a table top, then take the tiles directly from the table to the wall. By doing this, you will be able to see what the pattern looks like, and make any adjustments before the tiles are stuck down.

MAKING YOUR OWN MOSAIC

As well as standard, square mosaic tiles, you can use smaller and irregularly shaped tiles to create mosaics that are less uniform. Incorporate small pieces of broken tile to build up either simple patterns or more complicated images.

● **Making mosaic tiles** Use tile nibblers to break up old and leftover tiles into small irregular pieces approximately 2–4 cm² (¾–½ sq in) in area.
● **Producing a design** A design can be drawn on a wall using a similar method to that used for painting murals (see p. 36). Carefully fill in the shapes that make up the image with small pieces of tile instead of paint to create your own mosaic.

Creating a bold design
You can combine irregular-shaped fragments of tile with custom-made, square mosaic tiles to stunning effect. Framing the area with uniform but vivid bands of colour adds drama.

INSERTING TILES AND BORDERS

Picture tiles, inset tiles, and border tiles can provide the finishing touches on a tiled surface. They add interest to a plain tile design, or – in the case of borders – frame the whole tiled area or a panel. The choice of tiles is huge, so finding some suitable ones should be easy.

USING BORDER TILES

● **Ordering work** Always finish the main body of tiling before applying border tiles.
● **Applying tiles** Because most border tiles are by nature very narrow, spread the adhesive on the back of the tile and then position it on the wall, rather than applying adhesive to the wall before fixing the tile.
● **Dealing with corners** Mitring corners is difficult with a standard tile cutter, so flush-join the tiles, or calculate where the mitre cuts will be, and ask your supplier to cut them.
● **Tiling up to wallpaper** If you are papering a wall above a tiled area, insert the extreme edge of the paper beneath the tile edges. Complete the tiling as far as the border, then apply the paper to just below where the upper edge of the border tiles will be. Once the papering is complete, attach the border tiles in position.

INSERTING DADOS

● **Using wood** Vary the texture of a tiled surface by inserting a wooden moulding in the form of a dado rail. Paint it to match or complement the surrounding tiled area.

Using dado tiles
Create a dado effect within a tiled wall using flat tiles that provide a contrasting band of colour or pattern. Alternatively, insert precisely cut half-tiles in another colour or pattern to produce the same effect.

VARYING BORDERS

● **Offsetting joins** Many border tiles are a different width from the main tiles. Offset the joins when possible, so that they occur near the mid-point of the main tile width.

Deepening a border
Create a deep border by using two rows of border tiles one beneath the other. Place relief border tiles along the top, for example, with decorated border tiles below to create a more interesting decorative effect.

PLANNING TILED IMAGES

Drawing a plan
Using squared paper, draw an accurate plan to scale of the whole area to be tiled, including any picture tiles. Follow the plan carefully as you tile. This will help to ensure that picture tiles are positioned accurately.

INSERTING PICTURE TILES

● **Changing existing tiles** Rejuvenate an old tiled surface by removing some tiles and inserting picture tiles. Remove tiles by means of the technique used for replacing broken or cracked tiles (see p. 71).
● **Creating panels** Use picture tiles to make up separate tiled panels on suitable flat areas of wall, making a decorative feature that is not necessarily part of a larger tiled area.
● **Making a border** Create a deep border using picture tiles instead of border tiles. Use the opportunity to introduce a theme. A border of fruits and vegetables, for example, will be suitable for a kitchen.

MONEY-SAVING TIP

Adding new tiles to old
Attach a new tiled border above old bathroom tiles to spruce the room up without completely retiling. Clean up the old tiles thoroughly, and regrout if necessary.

TILING WORK SURFACES

Most wall tiles, as their name suggests, are applied to flat, vertical surfaces. However, horizontal surfaces are often just as eligible for tiling, and some can benefit greatly. The most common application is to cover work surfaces with tiles, such as in kitchens and utility rooms.

TILING HORIZONTALLY

- **Supporting weight** Tiles are relatively heavy, so if a work surface is lightweight, you may need to give it some additional support. The best way of doing this is to build up the top of the work surface with a sheet of plyboard to spread the extra weight.
- **Making surfaces ready** Many work surfaces are not suitable for tiling on to directly. To prepare such surfaces, cut out and fit a thin piece of plyboard or MDF as a base on which you can attach the tiles.
- **Neatening edges** Always use whole tiles along the front edge of a work surface, and work backwards to a cut join if necessary at the wall.

ADJUSTING GROUT

- **Finishing flush** Apply grout so that it is absolutely flush with the tiles. This will make it easier to clean the tiled surface, and reduce the risk of dirt lodging in grout crevices.
- **Cleaning grout** Use a proprietary grout cleaner from time to time to help keep the grouted areas of a tiled work surface as clean as possible.
- **Grouting hygienically** The most hygienic way of grouting tiles is with an epoxy-based grout. This forms a longer-lasting surface that is far more resistant to bacterial growth than traditional grout. Epoxy-based grout is difficult to apply, however, so you may need to hire a professional.

EDGING WORK SURFACES

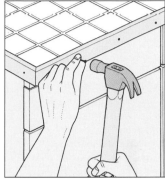

Attaching battens
Attach hardwood battens along work-surface edges to produce a neat finish. Paint or varnish as required. Make sure that the batten tops are flush with the tiles, otherwise cleaning the work surface will be difficult.

USING PURPOSE-MADE TILES

Besides their most obvious function of providing a tough washable surface, tiles have other practical uses around the home. Many types have been specially modified in design for a particular purpose, but ordinary tiles can also be put to a variety of uses.

SUPPORTING HEAVY TILES

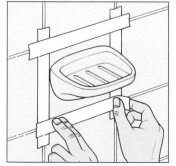

Attaching soap dishes
Because of its weight, a soap-dish tile needs support to stay in place while the adhesive dries. Strap masking tape over it and the adjacent tiles for support. Remove the tape once the adhesive has dried.

MODIFYING WORKTOPS

Making a chopping board
Cut a hole and insert a tile in a worktop to create a permanent chopping board. A large marble tile is ideal, since it is tough and easily cleaned. Seal around the edges of the tile with a bead of clear silicone after inserting it.

IMPROVING EFFICIENCY

- **Waterproofing showers** Tiles in a shower area will be heavily bombarded by water, and require extra waterproofing. Use a specialized, proprietary waterproofing grout, and seal all corners within the shower area with clear silicone after you have grouted to provide an extra waterproof barrier.
- **Tiling sills** Bathrooms are especially prone to high levels of condensation. Water run-off on to a sill can quickly degrade the surface if the sill is merely painted. It is a good idea, therefore, to tile all the sills in a bathroom to give them extra protection and increase their lifespan.

DECORATING PLAIN TILES

Completely retiling a room can be expensive, so it is always worth considering whether or not existing tiles can be renovated using other decorative methods. Similarly, you can buy inexpensive, plain tiles, and then enhance them using one or more painting techniques.

PAINTING TILES

● **Repairing grout** Rake out any old, loose grout from joints using a scraper, and fill the gaps with all-purpose filler.
● **Preparing surfaces** Prepare an old tiled surface by cleaning it down thoroughly with sugar soap and rinsing with clean water. Allow to dry thoroughly, then apply a proprietary tile primer.
● **Applying paint** After you have carried out the correct preparation, you can use either proprietary tile paints or normal acrylic or oil-based paints. Protect the tiles with a coat of ceramic varnish once you have finished painting.
● **Painting selectively** There is no need to paint all the tiles on a wall. Simply painting in a border or stencilling images on a few tiles can revive the look of a "tired" tiled surface.

HAND-PAINTING TILES

Using ceramic paints, you can paint your own designs on to tiles as long as they have been correctly prepared. Depending on the extent of your artistic capabilities, you can transfer an image to a tile and colour it in (as below), or paint it freehand.

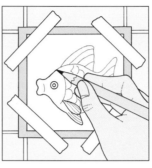

1 Use masking tape to stick an image over a tile, placing carbon paper between the image and the tile. Draw around the picture outline, pressing hard enough for the carbon to transfer the image to the tile.

2 Paint in the image, taking care not to apply too much paint and risk drips and runs. Add as much detail as you wish. Allow one colour to dry before applying any others, thus preventing them from running.

PAINTING TILES IN LOW-WEAR AREAS

If you do not use the correct materials, painted tiles will not wear well, since moisture and regular cleaning will damage the finish. In areas of low wear, however, painted surfaces will survive better, so you can substitute other materials.

● **Creating paint effects** Use an oil-based eggshell as a base coat for paint effects on tiles. Sponging and ragging are very effective. Finish off with a protective coat of varnish.
● **Using transfers** Proprietary tile transfers will brighten up and change the appearance of even the plainest tiled area.
● **Creating mosaics** Paint old tiles different colours, and break them up into pieces for a mosaic.

Using car paints
Car touch-up paints are ideal materials to use for painting small motifs or patterns on to a few tiles to brighten them up. You will not even need to find a brush, since this is usually an integral part of the container.

PROTECTING IMAGES

Applying varnish
Protect stencilled images (see p. 35) on tiles with ceramic varnish. There is no need to varnish the whole tile. Use the stencil to ensure that the varnish is applied to the image only.

FINISHING OFF

T ILES REQUIRE CARE AFTER APPLICATION to ensure that they look good and wear well for as long as possible. As well as tidying them up decoratively, you must finish off tiles so that they serve their practical purpose efficiently.

WATERPROOFING TILES

Tiles are of little practical use unless they are completely waterproofed, providing an easily cleaned surface that is totally impermeable to water. Joints and tile edges are the areas most prone to water penetration and seepage, and therefore require the most attention.

GROUTING SUCCESSFULLY

● **Selecting grout** Choose powdered grout that you mix with water, since this is more durable than dual-purpose adhesive or other grouts.
● **Making neat lines** Run a grout shaper or the edge of your finger down the joints once excess grout has been removed but before it dries.
● **Grouting marble tiles** Ensure that grout is flush with the tile surface to give the illusion of a flat expanse of marble.
● **Producing a sheen** Wipe the tiles first with a damp sponge to remove excess grout. When dry, polish with a lint-free cloth. Polish several times.

APPLYING GROUT

Using a grout spreader
Distribute grout with a spreader, which will not scratch a glazed surface and will push the grout firmly into every gap. Keep passing over the joints until the grout is completely compacted.

CHOOSING COLOUR

Matching grout
Grout is available in several different colours, so you can pick one to suit other decoration. Alternatively, mix white powdered grout with powdered pigments until you create the right colour.

SEALING WITH SILICONE

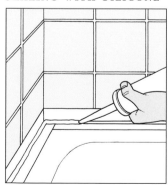

Filling a groove
Mask along a tile and the adjacent surface to make a straight-edged channel. Squeeze silicone into position from its tube. Smooth with a wetted finger, and remove the tape before the sealant dries.

USING PLASTIC STRIPS

● **Overlapping edges** Create a good seal by inserting custom-made plastic strips before you tile, so that the bottom edge of the bottom layer of tiles overlaps the top of the strip.
● **Double-sealing** Apply a bead of silicone behind a plastic strip as a double seal.
● **Dealing with corners** To create an effective water barrier at the same time as a mitred join, mitre only one plastic strip in a corner and lie it on top of the adjacent strip, which should run all the way into the corner flush to the tiles.
● **Attaching strips** Fix a strip to tiles and adjacent surfaces with waterproof, double-sided tape.

BRIGHT IDEA

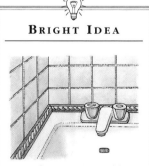

Using decorative mouldings
Wooden mouldings may be used as a seal along tile edges as long as the wood has been primed and painted with an oil-based paint. Fix the moulding in position using silicone sealant.

ATTACHING FITTINGS

Tiling is not complete until fixtures and fittings have been attached to the tiled surface. Tiled surfaces cannot be touched up in a similar manner to painted or wallpapered surfaces, so make sure that fittings are placed in the correct position at the first attempt.

DRILLING WISELY

● **Keeping to the middle** Try to position attachments so that you drill holes in tiles away from the edges. Drilling near edges may cause cracking.
● **Making watertight** When putting a screw into a hole in a tile, apply a small bead of silicone to the point of the screw. This will prevent any water from seeping into the hole and behind the tile.
● **Protecting eyes** Use goggles when drilling to protect your eyes from flying tile splinters.
● **Finding alternatives** If an attachment will have a low load-bearing function, use self-adhesive pads to fix it in place.

DRILLING HOLES

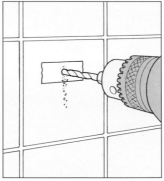

Preventing slippage
Place masking tape over the point at which a fitting will be attached, and drill through the tape into the wall. The tape will prevent the drill from slipping.

POSITIONING FITTINGS

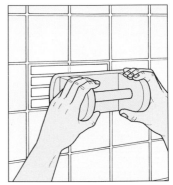

Using double-sided tape
Temporarily attach a fitting to the wall using double-sided tape. This will enable you to judge whether to make adjustments prior to fixing the fitting.

CLEANING UP

As with all decorating tasks, no tiling job is complete until the necessary cleaning up and tidying away has been done. The finished tile surfaces should be wiped down well, and all equipment should be thoroughly washed and dried, then stored away carefully and safely.

REMOVING DRIED GROUT

● **Using scourers** To remove very small pieces of dried grout from a newly tiled surface, rub gently with a dampened, non-abrasive kitchen scourer.

Using a window scraper
Remove dried grout with a window scraper, running the sharp edge of the blade smoothly over the tiles. To avoid scratching the glazed surface, lubricate the scraper with washing-up liquid.

TIDYING GROUT

● **Touching up grout** It may take a day or so for grout to dry completely, and during this time air bubbles may form in the grouted joints (especially beneath the lower edges of tiles). Pierce any bubbles, and fill the holes with small beads of grout applied with one finger.
● **Cleaning sanitary ware** To remove spots of dry grout from baths or basins, fill them with hot water, and allow the grout to soak. Run the water away, and wipe off the grout with a non-abrasive pad.
● **Cleaning carpet** If any tile adhesive or grout falls on to a carpet during tiling, allow it to dry before removing with a stiff-bristled brush.

BRIGHT IDEA

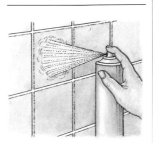

Sealing grout
Once grout has dried and tiles have been cleaned, spray the tiled surface with a silicone-based household polish. This will not only clean and polish the tiles, but it will also seal the grout and help maintain its colour.

MAINTAINING TILES

Tiles have a long decorative life which tends to end because colour preferences and design trends change rather than because of the deterioration of the tiles themselves. Sometimes, however, a little regular maintenance and a few repairs are needed to keep tiles looking pristine.

REPLACING AN ISOLATED DAMAGED TILE

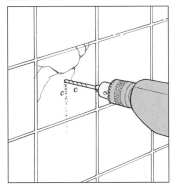

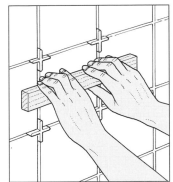

1 First, loosen the tile's adhesion to the wall. Do this by drilling several holes in the tile, thus breaking up the surface. Remember to wear goggles to protect your eyes.

2 With a hammer and bolster chisel, chip out fragments of tile, taking care not to crack adjacent tiles. Keep the goggles on; you may also wish to wear gloves to protect your hands.

3 Spread adhesive on the back of a new tile, and stick it in position. Use spacers to hold it there and a batten to make sure that it is flush with adjacent tiles. Grout and polish.

DEALING WITH CRACKS

● **Using paint** Mix a small amount of an artist's paint (which matches the tile colour) with grout to make a paste. Smooth it into small, hairline cracks to fill them. Clean away excess, then leave to dry.

KEEPING GROUT WHITE

● **Cleaning grout** Treat dirty grout with a proprietary grout cleaner or a mild solution of household bleach. Do a test patch to ensure that the tiles will not discolour. Work in with a toothbrush, then rinse off.

REPLACING GROUT

● **Starting over** Grout is prone to discolouration from dirt or simply through aging. Clear out old grout with a grout raker or the edge of a scraper, and regrout the whole tiled area as you would normally.

USING LEFTOVER TILES

Always keep some leftover tiles for replacement purposes. Trying to find a matching tile after a number of years is difficult. Even shades of white vary if different makes of tile are placed side by side. There are many ways of using up the rest of your leftover tiles.

● **Adding to the tiling plan** You can always add an additional row to an area that you have already tiled – for example, to increase the size of a tiled splashback. It is usually worth reconsidering the extent of the original tiling design.

● **Tiling sills** Areas of heavy wear, such as windowsills, benefit from tiling. Use leftovers from another project for this. You will create a more hardwearing, easily wiped, as well as attractive surface.
● **Making kitchen equipment** Attach a picture tile to a wooden block to make a cheese board. A large marble tile can be used as a chopping board. Attach rubber feet to prevent it slipping.
● **Using broken tiles** Broken tiles are useful for making mosaic tiles (see p. 65). Alternatively, shape the fragments with tile nibblers, and attach them to the rim of plant pots for extra decoration.

Cut down firmly into cork tile

Making a pot stand
Place a leftover picture tile squarely in the corner of a cork floor tile. Cut around the other two edges with a craft knife. Glue tile to cork with neat PVA.

DECORATING WOODWORK

*I*F THE WALLS ARE THE BACKDROP *for all the decorative features of a room, then the woodwork is the frame upon which the whole look of the room hangs. It is up to you how prominent you make that framework, which offers you great scope for experimentation. Decorating woodwork is not confined to permanent fixtures: painting furniture adds a further decorative dimension.*

SELECTING MATERIALS

There is great diversity in the types of finish available for wood. They vary considerably in terms of colour and sheen as well as their level of opacity and translucency. The choice of finish depends on the type of wood and how it fits in with other decorated surfaces.

PAINT TYPES AND WOOD FINISHES

TYPE	FINISH	USES	COVERAGE
Gloss/ Quick-drying (QD) gloss	Gloss is oil based with a high-gloss finish. It is extremely hardwearing. QD gloss is water based with a less shiny finish than standard gloss.	You can apply gloss to all woods. Use an oil-based primer on resinous woods. QD is suitable for all woods except resinous ones and is ideal for retouching.	17 m²/l (92 sq yd/gal) QD: 15 m²/l (82 sq yd/gal)
Eggshell/ Quick-drying (QD) eggshell	Hardwearing eggshell is oil based with a mid-sheen finish. Water-based QD eggshell has a mid-sheen finish. It is not as hardwearing as eggshell.	Eggshell is ideal on poor surfaces. QD is suitable for most woods, except highly resinous ones. Its quick-drying properties make it ideal for busy areas.	16 m²/l (87 sq yd/gal) QD: 15 m²/l (82 sq yd/gal)
Varnish/ Quick-drying (QD) varnish	Varnish is oil based with a matt to high-gloss finish. It is extremely hardwearing. Water-based QD varnish has a matt to gloss finish and is hardwearing.	Varnish is suitable for all woods. Smooth-planed surfaces produce the best finish. QD varnish is suitable for all woods and ideal for large-scale areas.	15 m²/l (82 sq yd/gal) QD: 10 m²/l (55 sq yd/gal)
Woodstain/ Quick-drying (QD) woodstain	Woodstain is oil based with a low- to high-sheen, translucent finish and is hardwearing. Water-based QD woodstain also has a translucent finish.	Woodstain can be applied to all woods (must be stripped) and is good for mixtures of wood. QD is suitable for all woods and allows several coats in a day.	22 m²/l (120 sq yd/gal) QD: 20 m²/l (110 sq yd/gal)
Scandinavian oil	Solvent-based, mid-sheen, nourishing finish.	Ideal for hardwoods and low-wear areas.	12 m²/l (65 sq yd/gal)
Wax	Solvent- or water-based finish that requires polishing.	Suitable for all woods. Can be applied over stains and dyes.	17 m²/l (92 sq yd/gal)

BASIC PAINTING EQUIPMENT

Equipment for painting wood is little different from that for painting walls, requiring just a few additional items.

● **Choosing brushes** Painting woodwork involves more detailed and smaller-scale work than painting walls, so you will need a larger range of small brushes. Pure bristle brushes give the highest-quality finish but are more expensive than their synthetic counterparts. They are, however, easier to use.

● **Selecting sandpaper** Buy several grades of sandpapers. A good-quality, fine-grade paper is essential for the smoothest possible finish.

Angle-head paintbrush

12.5-mm (½-in) paintbrush

Lint-free cloth

50-mm (2-in) paintbrush

Varnish brush

Sandpaper

Hot-air gun

Dust sheet

Small roller and tray

CALCULATING QUANTITIES

Measuring solid surfaces such as doors and skirting boards is relatively simple. With other items, a method of measuring up may not be obvious. Use the table opposite to calculate how much paint you need for surfaces of average porosity.

● **Windows** To calculate the surface area of the frame of a picture window, measure the frame's width and perimeter. Casement windows have many rails, so measure the area of the whole window, including the glass.

● **Coverage** Paints and natural-wood finishes vary in their coverage. Consider this carefully when calculating the number of coats required.

● **Preparatory coats** Do not forget that bare wood needs priming and most paints need an undercoat before painting.

WOOD TYPES COMMONLY FOUND AROUND THE HOME

Many types of wood are found around the average home. They are categorized according to suitability of finish.

● **Natural woods** You will find that planed wood is used generally for intricate areas such as architraves and skirting. Rough-sawn wood is used for construction and is unlikely to require decorating. The exception to this may be houses in which beams are exposed.

● **Manufactured woods** You may prefer to use "manufactured" woods, whose appearance differs greatly from natural grain. Produced in large sheets, the versatility of these materials means that they can be used for structural purposes, such as floors, as well as for making doors, panels, and other items. Some are impregnated with fire-retardant substances that may affect paint application.

Softwood
Natural wood, usually pale in colour. Used for all internal joinery. Takes most paints and natural-wood finishes.

Hardwood
Natural wood, higher quality than softwood. Used for internal joinery. Best suited to natural-wood finishes.

Plyboard
Sheets made of layers of veneer. Takes all paints but natural-wood finishes may give patchy coverage.

Medium-density fibreboard (MDF)
Sheets of compressed wood fibres. Often used for cupboards and door panels. Takes all paints.

Hardboard
Smooth, high-density board made of compressed wood fibres. Thinner than MDF; used for floors. Takes most paints.

Chipboard
Sheets of compressed wood particles. Often used as a flooring material. Takes certain paints – follow suppliers' guidelines.

PREPARING TO PAINT

Defects in woodwork tend to be enhanced rather than disguised by paint, so it is important to prepare the wood as well as possible before you paint it. Then make sure that you apply the paint using the appropriate techniques.

STRIPPING AND SANDING

You will have to judge how much preparation work is required and, more importantly, whether or not to remove old paint. Multiple layers are best stripped, but a previously sound painted surface can very often be redecorated after a thorough sand and wash down.

ORDER OF WORK

Use this checklist when planning your work. It may be varied slightly according to the paint system and manufacturers' guidelines.

- Mask adjacent surfaces.
- Strip old paint.
- Seal knots.
- Prime bare wood.
- Fill cracks and holes.
- Sand surfaces.
- Vacuum clean.
- Wipe down surfaces.
- Paint undercoat.
- Lightly sand.
- Wipe down.
- Paint top coat.

HEAT STRIPPING

Using a hot-air gun
Scrape off paint as it bubbles with a broad-bladed stripping knife. Do not apply heat for long in one place, since the wood may scorch. Use the scraper to protect the previously stripped area.

STRIPPING SAFELY

- **Protecting yourself** Always wear a respiratory mask to reduce the risk of inhaling harmful fumes given off by the paint or a chemical stripper. Also, you may like to protect your hands from injury or irritation by wearing gloves.
- **Reducing fire risks** Never leave a hot-air gun unattended while it is switched on.
- **Checking for lead** When stripping very old layers of paint, check that they do not contain lead, which is toxic if it gets into the body. Most builder's merchants sell lead tester kits for this purpose.

USING CHEMICALS

- **Applying stripper** Wear a pair of gloves, and use an old brush to apply stripper. Use a dabbing rather than a brushing motion. Do not brush the stripper in too much since this will reduce its concentration over that area.
- **Stripping outside** Stripping can be a messy business, so if possible remove doors and strip them outdoors. Lay them horizontally on trestles so that a thick coat of stripper can be applied without running off.
- **Neutralizing stripper** Once old paint has been removed, neutralize the chemicals in the stripper by washing down the wood with white vinegar. Then rinse with clean water.

SANDING MOULDINGS

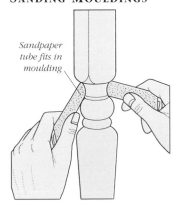

Sandpaper tube fits in moulding

Using a sandpaper tube
To make sanding intricate areas such as bannister mouldings easier, roll up some sandpaper into a tube. Adjust the diameter of the tube so that it matches the rounded profile of the moulding.

TRADITIONAL TIP

Wiping down
Before painting a horizontal surface, wipe it with a lint-free cloth dampened with white spirit. This will pick up dust and smooth the finish ready for painting.

FILLING

Most woodwork cannot be simply sanded then painted. Usually scratches and small holes will need some filling prior to painting. There are a variety of fillers available for this: some are all-purpose, while others, such as fine surface filler, serve a specific purpose.

FOLLOWING GUIDELINES

● **Removing dust** Once an area has been filled and sanded, remove any filler dust by wiping with a damp cloth.
● **Saving time** Keep a pot of ready-mixed filler handy for filling small holes that you may have missed the first time.
● **Smoothing surfaces** Use a fine surface filler on ornate mouldings. When sanded, this will provide the smoothest possible surface for paint.
● **Moulding filler** Smooth filler into position when repairing small holes and cracks by shaping it with a damp artist's brush. Smoothing the filler carefully will reduce the need for sanding once it has dried.

DEALING WITH BIG GAPS

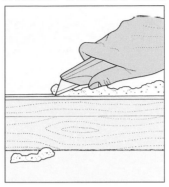

Filling and trimming
Use an aerosol foam filler to fill a large hole, such as a wide crack behind a skirting board. Traditional fillers will not hold in place as well. Trim any excess filler with a craft knife.

USING FLEXIBLE FILLER

● **Raking out** Remove flaky paint and other pieces of debris from cracked joints by running the edge of a scraper firmly down the joint. Dust out before applying the filler.
● **Smoothing** Tubed flexible filler cannot be sanded, so smooth it before it dries. Once the filler is in position, use a clean, damp sponge to smooth it over. To give the best finish, run down the joint with a wetted finger.
● **Preventing cracking** Hairline cracks may appear in water-based paint applied over flexible filler. Avoid these by priming the filler with oil-based undercoat before painting.

PRIMING AND PAINTING

In order to produce the best finish, consider carefully any preparatory coats and the top coats that will be required. These will differ depending on whether you have chosen water- or oil-based materials. Also think about the techniques suitable for painting wooden surfaces.

APPLYING FIRST COATS

● **Sealing knots** Apply a white knotter when using a water-based paint system. It will be more compatible with acrylic paints, and will seal knots without showing through subsequent coats of paint.
● **Coating natural wood** When applying a natural-wood system, do not knot or prime. Most natural wood coatings will automatically be sealed when you apply the first coat.
● **Breaking in brushes** Always use new brushes for priming rather than painting, since they will probably moult bristles the first time they are used. This means they will be in a better condition for applying subsequent coats.

APPLYING TOP COATS TO FLAT SURFACES

1 First, paint a number of vertical strips about 30 cm (12 in) in length. Reload the brush with paint for each strip. Without reloading, spread the paint across the panel surface using horizontal strokes.

2 Without reloading, lightly brush the area vertically to lay off the paint and produce an even coverage. Use this technique for painting both undercoats and top coats on most flat surface areas.

PAINTING SPECIFIC AREAS

Y OUR PAINTING TECHNIQUE will always have to be adapted to suit different areas and surfaces. Most adaptations will be concerned with the order in which an area is painted, and obtaining the best finish quickly and efficiently.

PAINTING DOORS

D oors make up the largest proportion of wooden surfaces in most homes, and it is therefore important that they are painted in the right way. Door designs vary, but most common ones fall into two categories – panelled or flat – in terms of technical painting requirements.

PAINTING DOORS TO REFLECT ROOM COLOURS

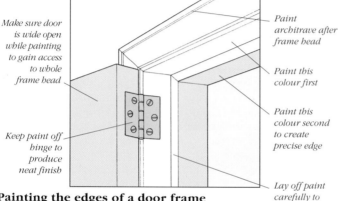

Make sure door is wide open while painting to gain access to whole frame head

Keep paint off hinge to produce neat finish

Paint architrave after frame head

Paint this colour first

Paint this colour second to create precise edge

Lay off paint carefully to avoid excess forming drip marks along frame edge

Painting the edges of a door frame
If two different-coloured rooms adjoin at a doorway, you need to delineate clearly where the colour of one room ends and the colour of the other room begins. Following convention, paint certain edges within a door frame one colour or the other in order to indicate which room they belong to decoratively.

DEFINING EDGES

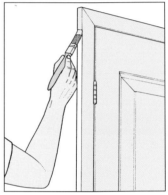

Resting your elbow
Facilitate the painting of straight lines between architrave and wall by resting your elbow against the wall. As you move the paintbrush down, your hand will be less likely to wobble.

PAINTING CUPBOARDS

Consider these points when painting cupboards to save time and increase efficiency.

● **Removing door furniture** Remove handles and door catches to make painting easier and prevent them from being splashed with paint.
● **Painting drawers** Paint the fronts of drawers but not the sides and runners, since this will hinder drawer motion.
● **Painting inside** Paint a pale colour inside a cupboard to increase light reflection when the door is open. You will then see the contents more easily.

COVERING DOORS EFFICIENTLY

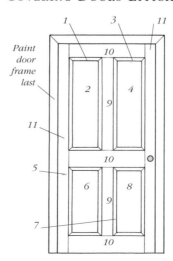

Paint door frame last

● **Opening and closing** Save time by removing door furniture before painting. It is difficult to move a door with no handle, so wedge it open with folded card while painting, and use a screwdriver as a handle.

Working to order
Paint the panels of a door in a logical sequence (1–11). Starting at the top, and working from left to right, paint in narrow, horizontal sections. Use a small brush to paint mouldings and for cutting in. Paint a flat door in 0.25-m² (2.5-sq-ft) sections from top to bottom and left to right.

PAINTING WINDOWS

You may be concerned that painting around panes of glass is both difficult and time-consuming. This does not have to be the case, however, if you paint windows in a systematic way and extend your repertoire of painting techniques slightly to aid the process further.

PLANNING THE PAINTING OF WINDOWS

● **Starting early** Paint windows early in the day so that they can stay open to dry for as long as possible. Wedge them open with card to prevent them from slamming shut.

Paint precise lines between wood and wall

● **Cleaning glass** Remove splashes of undercoat with a window scraper and polish the glass with a proprietary household cleaner before top-coating the woodwork.

Working logically
Work from the top of a window frame downwards, and from areas nearest the glass outwards (1-6). Follow this system to ensure that you do not miss any part of the frame. It is easy to miss areas if the new paint colour is similar to the old.

SHIELDING GLASS

Using a window guard
Cut the base out of a plastic food container, leaving part of one side as a handle. Hold the guard to the glass-rebate junction, and paint without overspill on to the glass. Clean the guard regularly.

PAINTING OTHER AREAS

Not all the surfaces around a home fit into simple categories: some will require more diverse techniques. Metal surfaces, for example, might require specific preparation before you decorate them, and certain parts of the house, such as high-wear areas, need special attention.

DEALING WITH METAL

● **Removing rust** Patches of rust should be sanded – right back to the bare metal if necessary. Prime and paint immediately to prevent moist air from getting at the bare surface and triggering the rusting process once again.
● **Choosing primers** You might find a vast array of different metals and alloys around your home. Make sure that you use a primer that suits each metal's individual properties.
● **Painting radiators** Always paint radiators when they are cold. Applying paint to a warm or hot surface will cause it to dry too quickly. The paint will therefore be difficult to brush out, resulting in a patchy finish.

NEGOTIATING PIPES

● **Painting large pipes** Use a radiator roller to cover large pipes quickly and evenly. Protect nearby areas from overspray. Cut in with a brush.

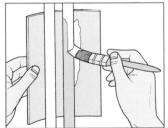

Shielding a wall
To make it easier to paint pipes that are against a wall, hold a piece of card behind them to protect the wall from a build-up of paint splashes. Move the card up or down as you progress.

PAINTING STAIRWAYS

When painting woodwork on a stairway, consider the specific requirements of this part of the building. A good finish is especially important if the stairs are in constant use.

● **Protecting handrails** Give handrails an extra top coat, since these are the areas that receive the most wear.
● **Painting edges** Before laying a new carpet, cut in carefully on each step so that the painted area extends well beyond the carpet edge.
● **Filling cracks** Staircases are prone to slight movement, so use flexible filler in gaps and joints to prevent paintwork from cracking. You will thus produce a longer-lasting finish.

ENHANCING WOOD

YOU MAY DECIDE THAT KEEPING WOODEN SURFACES LOOKING NATURAL is a preferable option to painting or decorating them. There is a large range of finishes at your disposal, and many of them are easy to use, as well as being hardwearing.

SELECTING WOOD FINISHES

Natural-wood finishes can transform a lifeless wooden object into a vibrant decorative feature. Choose a finish according to the type of wood, and the colour and durability required. Water-based finishes are easy to apply; oil-based products are more hardwearing.

Oil
Suitable for dark hardwoods, as it is a subtle, highlighting finish. Buff up to create a sheen.

Wax
Most natural finish; enhances grain and texture. Buff up for sheen. Needs frequent recoating.

Varnish
Hardest-wearing: use alone or as tough top coat on other finishes. Sheen varies from matt to gloss.

Wood dye
Colours wood to whatever shade required. Colours can be mixed. Finish off with clear varnish.

Stain
Largest colour range and great depth of finish, which varies according to the number of coats.

USING WOOD FINISHES

Natural-wood finishes will enable you to match solid wooden fixtures in a room with pieces of furniture, or to make several different types of wood match each other. You can even make pine surfaces resemble oak, or transform deal so that it looks like mahogany.

TAKING CARE
● **Protecting yourself** Many wood finishes are runny, and spattering is unavoidable. Wear goggles, especially when coating at eye level.
● **Decanting** Always decant natural-wood finishes into a metal paint kettle. The surfaces of plastic containers might be damaged by these products.

SAFETY
Dispose of oily rags in a metal container with a lid. Oil is highly combustible, and there is a danger that rags might combust spontaneously.

IMPROVING FINISH
● **Using a sponge** Apply wood dye with a household sponge, thus eliminating the possibility of unsightly brush marks.
● **Buffing up easily** Attach a clean duster to the pad of an electric sander, and use to buff up a waxed or oiled surface.
● **Smoothing varnished coats** Use wire wool to rub down varnish after each coat. Remove residue with a lint-free cloth dampened with white spirit.
● **Staining evenly** Never stop halfway through staining a surface, otherwise an overlap mark will gradually become visible as subsequent coats of stain are applied.

GREEN TIP

Crush fruit with metal spoon

Using natural dyes
Liquidize fruits or vegetables with a little hot water, and strain to extract their natural dyes. Apply several coats, and seal with a coat of varnish.

CREATING PAINT EFFECTS

As well as having a considerable decorative impact, paint effects can be fun to do and they allow you to experiment with different paint finishes. Adapt the various effects so that you can stamp your individuality upon your home.

ADDITIONAL PAINTING EQUIPMENT

Much of the equipment used for creating paint effects on walls can be used for woodwork. Many tools are multi-purpose.

● **Including brushes** Include a variety of sizes of brush in your toolkit to cater for different surface areas and finishes.
● **Meeting specific requirements** A tool such as a rocker will enable you to produce a highly individual wood effect.

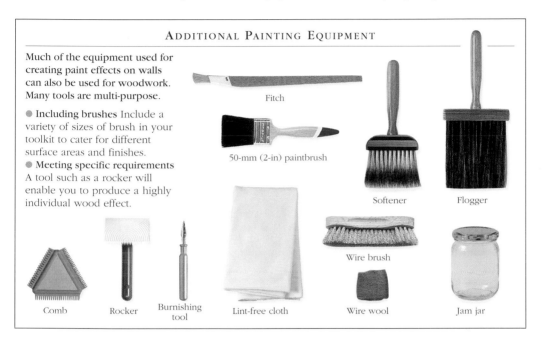

Fitch

50-mm (2-in) paintbrush

Softener

Flogger

Wire brush

Comb

Rocker

Burnishing tool

Lint-free cloth

Wire wool

Jam jar

MIMICKING NATURAL WOOD

The invention of a graining tool, or rocker, has revolutionized the creation of realistic natural-wood effects using a glaze (see p. 31). The choice of colours is virtually unlimited, so you can select natural, authentic wood tones or base your effects on bolder, brighter colours.

GRAINING WOOD
● **Choosing base colours** Create a solid feel by using a light base colour beneath a dark top coat. For greater depth and translucency, use a light top coat over a darker base.
● **Cleaning a rocker** Remove excess glaze from the tooling part of a rocker at regular intervals to prevent smudging.
● **Creating knots** Improve the texture of a wood finish by creating a few knots here and there. Do this by rolling the rocker tool backwards and forwards gently as you draw it across the glazed surface.

GRAINING KITCHEN CUPBOARD DOORS

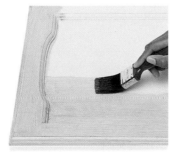

1 Take a cupboard door off, and lay it flat to make work easier. Apply a base coat such as eggshell, and let it dry. Apply a glaze evenly over the door using a 50-mm (2-in) brush.

2 While the glaze is wet, pull a rocker across the surface in vertical strokes to create a "grain". Do not stop mid-way, since glaze dries quickly and joins will show.

COLOURING WOOD

The simplest way of colouring wood is to colourwash it, using a technique similar to the one applied to walls (see p. 31). Liming wax offers an alternative and provides greater texture and depth. As well as colouring the wood, both these methods highlight the natural grain.

RAISING WOOD GRAIN

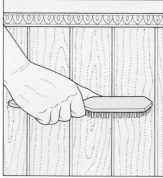

Using a wire brush
Stroke a wooden surface with a wire brush to open up the fibres that make up the grain. This will allow the surface to absorb more liming wax. Brush the wood gently, otherwise you might make indentations in the surface.

APPLYING LIMING WAX

● **Covering totally** To ensure that liming wax gets into all the nooks and grooves in a wooden surface, use a circular brushing motion when you apply the wax. Use a fairly stiff-bristled brush, which will force the wax into these gaps.
● **Removing excess** Once you have applied liming wax, rub a clear wax over the wooden surface using a lint-free cloth. This will both clean away any excess liming wax and provide a protective coating.
● **Buffing up** Once a wax coating has dried, give the wooden surface a final buff-up with a soft-bristled brush. A clean shoe-polishing brush is ideal for this purpose.

COLOURWASHING

Apply diluted paint or glaze to bare wood for a coloured, grain-enhancing finish.

● **Making a wash** For a simple wash, dilute ordinary matt emulsion with water until it has a milk-like consistency.
● **Rubbing back** Before a wash dries, rub the surface with a rag to remove excess paint and expose the grain, which will be highlighted.
● **Rough-sawn washing** Apply undiluted emulsion to rough-textured wood, allow to dry, then sand carefully with an electric sander. This will remove paint from the peaks but not the troughs, creating a colourwashed effect.

DRAGGING

Dragging is considered to be one of the more traditional paint effects, giving a wooden surface a textured look that tends to "lift" the finish, creating a realistic impression of depth. The technique is relatively simple, yet it can transform a flat wooden surface.

CREATING THE EFFECT

● **Varying texture** Vary texture by adjusting the angle at which you drag a brush across a glazed surface. Having the bristles at a steep angle to the wood produces a fine texture, whereas a shallow angle makes strokes coarser.
● **Using other tools** It is not essential to use a dragging brush, so experiment with other tools to vary the effect.
● **Dividing areas** Treat different sections of a door or different lengths of skirting, for example, as separate entities. It is important to drag continuously in the direction of the grain, and end strokes at junctions, joints, or natural divides.

DRAGGING A GLAZE

Using a brush
Apply an even coat of glaze, then draw a brush slowly across the glazed surface at a constant speed and with the bristles parallel to the grain. Do not stop until you have dragged the whole extent. Mask adjacent areas if necessary.

IMPROVISING TOOLS

Use sharp scissors to cut through rubber

Adapting a window scraper
Produce a dragged effect using a large car window scraper. Cut out sections of the tough rubber blade, making a jagged edge. Use the scraper in the same way as a brush. Because of its size, it will be suitable for large areas.

CREATING A METALLIC FINISH

Traditional painting materials can be used to create the impression of a metallic surface. There are products now available, however, that actually contain the metal that they are emulating. These materials produce a highly realistic metallic finish on a wooden surface.

CREATING VERDIGRIS

● **Selecting a surface** If you want to create the impression of verdigris, choose a wooden surface that includes patterned mouldings or other intricate details. This will make it easier for the surface to hold the colours, as well as ensuring a good range of colour shading across the area to be effected.

● **Choosing a subject** Consider creating a verdigris effect on an area or item that could well be made of metal, so that the deception is believable.

● **Building up colour** Use at least three shades of green as you build up a verdigris effect, the first verging on pale blue.

● **Sponging on** Apply layers of colour with a natural sponge, allowing one coat almost to dry before you apply another. Soften the sponged effect with a crumpled rag. This will expose the base coat in some places, adding authenticity.

HIGHLIGHTING IN GOLD

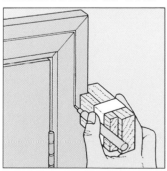

"Gilding" an architrave
Tape together a gold outliner pen and two blocks of wood, one of which slots around the architrave. The blocks will steady the pen and help you draw a straight, "gilded" line equidistant from the edge all the way around.

ESTABLISHING COLOUR

● **Painting a base colour** To increase the realism of a verdigris effect, choose a bronze- or copper-coloured paint for the base colour.

Dust powder by lightly tapping surface with bag

"Weathering" verdigris
Secure white, powdered filler within a muslin square. Before the last top coat dries, dust it with filler. The surface will then resemble weathered copper.

FAKING METALS

● **Leading** Apply a base coat of iron-oxide paint, then highlight the surface edges with black and dark-grey spray-paints. Spray a fine mist rather than covering the edges totally.

● **Choosing a hammered finish** Use a proprietary paint intended to give a textured, hammered finish on exterior metalwork to create a similar finish on interior woodwork.

● **Enamelling** Enamel paints mimic real metal effectively. Apply them to moulded skirting or doors to add detail.

● **Using car paints** Many cars have a metallic finish. Use a touch-up spray-paint in an appropriate colour to create metal effects on inside surfaces. Wear a mask when spraying.

USING METALLIC PAINT

Some proprietary metallic paints produce a highly authentic finish. They do not require any special preparation, and – with a certain amount of specialist finishing off – achieve very impressive results.

1 Metal paint can be applied directly to bare wood. A primer is advisable but not essential. Apply two coats of metal paint to create a totally opaque finish. Allow to dry overnight before proceeding.

2 Once the paint is dry, rub over the entire surface with a burnishing tool. Burnish in all directions over the surface, then buff up with wire wool. This takes time, but the quality of the effect warrants the effort.

MARBLING

There are many ways of producing a fake marble finish, largely because of the fact that the surface of natural marble varies greatly, depending on the type. Your main aim should be to reproduce the cloudy integration of different colours that is common to all marbles.

MARBLING PANELS USING A RAG

Apply glaze with soft brush

Flick rag on to wet glaze all over panel

1 Having let a base coat dry, randomly cover each panel with two colours of glaze. Apply the second colour before the first is dry; it does not matter if the colours run, since this will add to the effect.

2 Holding a damp, lint-free rag by one corner, flick it on to the glazed surface, thus mixing the colours. Work diagonally over each panel. Remove excess glaze from panel edges with a dry cloth.

INCREASING REALISM

● **Veining** Apply slightly diluted burnt umber with a fine-tipped artist's brush to suggest the veins characteristic of marble. Use a photograph or piece of marble as a guide. Drag the brush lightly in the same direction each time.
● **Softening** Soften a surface before the glaze dries. If you do not have a softening brush, use a soft dusting brush gently to blur the hard edges of "veins" or the base colours.
● **Protecting** Apply several protective coats of varnish to the finished product. A satin or mid-sheen varnish will create the most realistic finish.

COMBING

Combing is similar to dragging or graining, except that it offers greater diversity. You do not have to apply a combed pattern in the same direction as the wood grain. You will find that the creation of extravagant patterns is a very satisfying part of the combing technique.

COMBING EFFECTIVELY

● **Preparing surfaces** Combed designs look most effective when glaze lines are smooth. Prepare surfaces well so that they are perfectly level and free from depressions and lumps that would interfere with the comb's movement.
● **Choosing tools** Although you can buy specifically designed combing tools to create this effect, experiment with a notched grout spreader or traditional hair combs to introduce variety to the finish.
● **Creating combed designs** Choose from a number of designs created by combing. Basket weave, circles, or combinations of patterns, and images such as scrolls and lettering all look very effective.

CREATING PATTERNS ON A PANELLED DOOR

1 Decorate a panelled door in sections. Glaze and comb the horizontal rails first, then the vertical rails. The combing tool will make the rails look grained, in contrast with the door panels.

2 Now apply glaze to the panels. Keep the combed pattern symmetrical by maintaining a constant hand motion. After each combing movement, remove excess glaze from the comb's teeth.

PAINTING FURNITURE

MANY OF THE PAINT EFFECTS used on woodwork may also be applied to furniture. Some, however, are especially suitable for furniture, mainly because they require great attention to detail and are labour intensive.

PREPARING SURFACES

Many pieces of furniture are smaller scale than other wooden surfaces, and their surfaces may include fine details and curves. You may, therefore, have to spend more time preparing the surfaces thoroughly. However, the surface area will not be as extensive.

MAKING FURNITURE READY TO PAINT

Choose and prepare furniture carefully before painting it.

● **Choosing non-wooden items** Prepare and prime wicker or metal surfaces before painting.
● **Masking vulnerable items** With semi-upholstered items of furniture, mask the edges between wood and fabric.
● **Testing laminates** Do a test patch on laminated items. Many will not accept paint.

FILLING HOLES

Ensuring smoothness
Use a proprietary fine-surface filler for repairs, and apply with the end of one finger. Once sanded, this will produce a smoother finish than all-purpose filler.

PREPARING WOOD
● **Getting professional help** Hand-stripping old painted furniture can be difficult and time consuming, so take items to professional stripping firms where they can be acid dipped. The expense will be worth it.
● **Sanding** Use only fine-grade paper to sand furniture. Heavy sanding can easily distort furniture profiles and mouldings.
● **Preparing detailed surfaces** Apply several base coats to curved and detailed furniture surfaces before creating effects.

GILDING

As well as being very expensive, authentic gilding or water-gilding is a highly skilled craft that demands years of practice. Modern substitutes, such as Dutch metal, reduce costs dramatically and, if you apply an oil-based size, do not require special application skills.

APPLYING DUTCH METAL TO A FRAME

Size tinted with burnt umber

Apply size with paintbrush

Use small brush to push metal into crevices

Backing

1 Base-coat a frame, and let it dry. Apply gold size evenly all over. Tint the size with a little burnt umber so that you can see which areas have been covered. Allow the surface to dry until it is tacky.

2 Gently position the sheets of Dutch metal, metal-side down. Fit them around the moulding with a soft brush. Remove the backing, leaving the metal. When the size is dry, dust away excess metal.

MONEY-SAVING TIP

Using enamel paint
Produce a gilded effect inexpensively using gold enamel paint. Apply it very sparingly with a fitch to the edges of chair mouldings.

AGING

There are many different ways of making a piece of furniture look old. These techniques are known collectively as distressing, and they involve the use of various decorative materials aimed at creating a look that occurs naturally only after years of continuous wear and tear.

AGING EFFECTIVELY

● **Using emulsions** Use water-based paints, especially matt emulsions, which are much easier to distress than their oil-based equivalents. Their duller finish will give a more realistic impression of age.

● **Knocking about** Any piece of furniture with a history will have received the odd knock here and there. Randomly tap a screwdriver or chisel end over a wooden surface to create a well-worn effect.

● **Paying attention to edges** Make sure that you distress the edges of the object well, since this is where the most wear would have occurred.

● **Making details consistent** Exchange new handles on cupboards and cabinets for old ones. Dent metal door knobs with a hammer, and sand around the edges to imitate years of handling.

DISTRESSING WOODEN DOOR PANELS

● **Masking areas to be aged** Mask areas that are likely to have been worn with scraps of masking tape. Remove the tape once you have painted.

1 Use petroleum jelly to mask the areas that you wish to distress on a base-coated surface that has dried. Use just enough to "resist" the paint before painting the top coat.

ANTIQUING WOOD

● **Using wax** Brush liquid wax on to a painted or distressed surface, and buff up with wire wool. The wax will produce an apparently dirt-ingrained finish. Use an old toothbrush to reach into fiddly areas.

● **Applying wood dye** Use a soft cloth to apply wood dye (medium or dark oak). It has a similar effect to wax, but is more suitable on eggshell, which is oil-based, than water-based paints. Use sparingly.

● **Crackling successfully** To maximize the effectiveness of crackle varnish, ensure that the period of time between applying base-coat varnish and top-coat varnish is constant across the entire surface area.

● **Sanding** Use sandpaper to complete a distressed finish. Use flat sandpaper rather than a block so that you can judge how much pressure to apply.

2 Remove the paint-covered petroleum jelly using sandpaper. Sand the surface again to take the wood back to its natural finish, which will add authenticity to the effect.

HIGHLIGHTING CRACKS

Using artist's paint
To accentuate a crackle-varnish finish, rub in a darker artist's colour (such as burnt umber) to make the cracks more obvious. This is essential if you want to produce a good, delicately cracked, or *craquelure*, finish.

TIME-SAVING TIP

Using a hairdryer
A hairdryer will speed up the drying time of paint, allowing you to apply the next coat sooner. It is particularly useful when using crackle varnish, since the heat will also increase the size of the cracks.

APPLYING *DÉCOUPAGE*

Create the impression of a detailed, hand-painted surface without using any paint by applying the simple method of *découpage*. This involves cutting out appropriate images from a variety of sources – such as magazines – and attaching them to an object or piece of furniture.

DÉCOUPAGING SMALL CUPBOARDS

PVA

Acrylic varnish

1 Carefully cut out the images of your choice, and stick them down using PVA. Brush more PVA over the images to secure them. The thinner the paper used, the greater the impression of painted images.

2 Once the adhesive has dried, apply acrylic varnish to seal and protect the images. The more varnish you apply, the greater the hand-painted feel. Crackle varnish will emphasize this even more.

TRADITIONAL TIP

Sealing with egg tempera
Separate and break the yolk of an egg. Add a teaspoonful of distilled water and the same measure of linseed oil, and mix. Apply with a brush. Once dry, buff up with cotton wool.

CREATING ADVANCED EFFECTS

To produce advanced effects on furniture, you can employ the same basic techniques as you would to create other paint effects. However, you will have to pay more attention to detail and authenticity to mimic natural substances such as marble or tortoiseshell.

FAKING OTHER SURFACES

● **Hand-painting designs** Stencil images on to furniture. Create a hand-painted finish by going over the designs with an artist's brush, varying the detail and colour just enough to give it a freehand feel.
● **Graining accurately** Have an example of the wood you are imitating in front of you. This will make it easier to colour-match and copy the subtle grain variations of the wood.
● **Using *découpage*** Create the effect of tortoiseshell or marble by finding examples in books or magazines (which are out of copyright) and using a photocopier to enlarge them to the size you want. Apply using *découpage* techniques.

PERFECTING THE ART OF PRETENCE

● **Paying attention to detail** *Trompe l'oeil* effects do not have to be complicated and difficult to execute. You can create just as much impact with small details as large images.

● **Extending *trompe l'oeil*** Do not limit your use of *trompe l'oeil* effects to walls. With a little imagination, you can apply deceptive images to pieces of furniture, too.

Being practical
Paint a clever *trompe l'oeil* tablecloth on a garden table, and you will never again have to cover it before you lay the table. This simple yet striking image serves a very useful purpose, but at the same time does not require a high level of artistic skill.

FINISHING OFF

W HEN FINISHING OFF WOODWORK DECORATION, make sure that all necessary retouching is carried out. When the work is complete, clean equipment, then store it carefully. Finally, maintain painted surfaces to prolong their life.

CORRECTING MISTAKES

E xpect to do a certain amount of mistake-rectifying before you store your equipment away. Even experienced decorators sometimes have to retouch or even repaint some areas. Take time to make improvements and thus ensure that the finish is as good as possible.

REMOVING FLAWS
● **Drips** Shave off drips with a window scraper, and sand so that the whole area is flat. Undercoat and top-coat.
● **Brush marks** A few brush marks are inevitable. Those that appear grooved should be dealt with. Sand the whole area, first with rough paper, then smooth. Wipe and recoat.
● **Patchy finishes** Patches or shaded areas indicate either poor coverage or inadequate mixing of paint. In either case, remix top-coat paint properly, and apply another coat.

DEALING WITH BLEEDING

Removing resin
Improperly prepared knots may suffer from resinous bleeding, spoiling a top coat of paint. Use a hot-air gun to bubble out all the resin. Remove the resin with a scraper. Prime and recoat.

SMOOTHING SURFACES
● **Grit and dust** Dirt can get into brushes, and from them on to painted surfaces. If this occurs, sand lightly and recoat.
● **Orange-peel effect** Wrinkles are caused by oil-based paint being applied over paint that has not dried or that dries too quickly – in direct sunlight, for example. Strip and repaint.
● **Insect invasions** Insects are attracted to paint and stick to a tacky surface. Allow paint to dry, then wipe away insects with a dry cloth. Sand lightly, and recoat if necessary.

CLEANING UP

C lean up thoroughly after completing a job, firstly to ensure that the work looks its best, and secondly to make sure that tools and equipment are kept in good working order. Oil-based paints are commonly used on wood, and these especially need to be cleaned up well.

REMOVING DRY PAINT

Gently force comb through encrusted bristles

Combing a paintbrush
Use a grooming comb or a metal household comb to break up caked-on paint. The bristles can then be cleaned more easily, and will remain flexible in the future.

CLEANING PROPERLY
● **Cleaning hands** Use a proprietary hand cleaner rather than spirit-based products, which may irritate the skin.
● **Cleaning according to type** Use plain water for cleaning up acrylic paints, and white spirit for oil-based paints. Read the labels on specialist proprietary products carefully, since they may require thinners or other products.
● **Dealing with stubborn paint** Suspend a brush in solvent overnight to loosen paint. Do not let the bottom of the bristles touch the base of the container.

GREEN TIP

Reusing white spirit
Remove paint sediment from white spirit by sieving the solvent into another jar. This will prevent sediment getting into brushes as you clean them.

STORING MATERIALS

Not all the materials that you buy for a decorating job will be totally used up, so you will have to store leftovers. All pieces of equipment must be cleaned thoroughly before being stored so that they are kept in good working order until you need them again.

DEALING WITH PAINT

● **Decanting water-based paints**
Transfer leftover water-based paints into small jars to save space during storage. Use them to tint glazes for paint effects, or as samples when you are trying to decide upon a new colour scheme in the future.

● **Combining oil-based paints**
Pour leftover oil-based paints into one can, and mix them together for storage. Use the mixture on surfaces where colour is not important, such as the inside of exterior metal guttering to prevent corrosion.

● **Keeping tubes together**
Store tubes of artist's colour together in a clean paint can so that you do not lose them.

PROTECTING BRISTLES

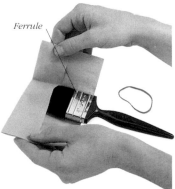

Ferrule

Maintaining shape
Wrap the bristle end of a clean brush in brown paper. Secure with a rubber band around the ferrule to protect and maintain bristle shape during storage.

STORING SMALL BRUSHES

Lie all brushes the same way

Taping brushes together
Small brushes can easily be lost. Bind them together with masking tape, thus making several small objects into one large one, which will be more difficult to lose.

MAINTAINING WOODWORK

Like other decorated surfaces, woodwork needs a certain amount of care to maintain it in the best possible condition. Following a few simple guidelines will make a finish long-lasting. A little effort from time to time will prevent a lot more effort in the long term.

REVIVING SURFACES

● **Maintaining coats** Apply the occasional coat of varnish to appropriate wooden surfaces to revive and protect the finish.

● **Retouching marks** Paint can become affected by natural light only a few months after decorating, with the result that its colour changes slightly from the original shade. When retouching a mark on a wall, make sure that you paint a wider area. If you need to retouch a door panel, cover the whole panel so that no colour differences become visible across the surface.

● **Cleaning surfaces** Clean most wood finishes simply with a damp sponge and mild household detergent.

REDECORATING WINDOW FRAMES

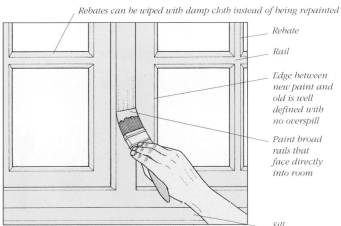

Rebates can be wiped with damp cloth instead of being repainted

Rebate

Rail

Edge between new paint and old is well defined with no overspill

Paint broad rails that face directly into room

Sill

Repainting selectively
Repaint only the rails and sills of a window frame rather than the entire frame. Rails are the most visible areas, and sills need regular maintenance. Avoid fiddly rebates, thus speeding up the job. Use the same colour paint as the original finish.

COVERING FLOORS

F*LOORING IS WITHOUT DOUBT the most practical aspect of home decoration and clearly has a dual-purpose function. Practical considerations and decorative choices are both equally important. Make sure that flooring options are not an afterthought once you have completed all the other decoration in a room. Such a large surface area contributes significantly to the total decorative look and deserves careful thought at the same time as you choose other decorative materials.*

BASIC FLOORING EQUIPMENT

Much of the equipment needed for flooring is already a part of most household toolkits.

● **Hiring specialist tools** Hire specialist equipment if you need it. It is usually expensive, and you are unlikely to use it enough to justify buying.
● **Checking hired equipment** Make sure that equipment is working and has all necessary operating instructions and safety recommendations.
● **Planning tool use** Plan work so that you hire equipment only when you need it. Do not hire an item on day one if you will not require it until day three.

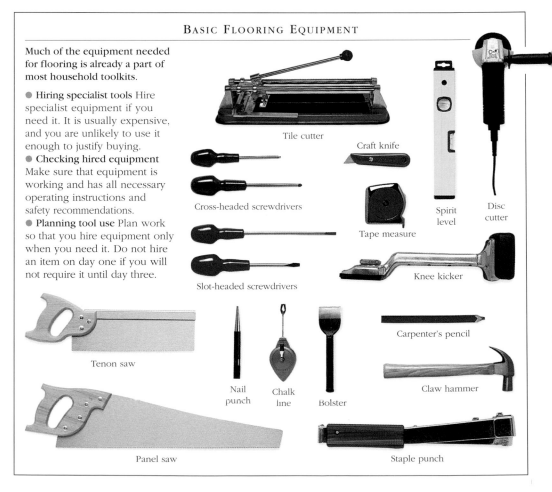

Tile cutter

Craft knife

Cross-headed screwdrivers

Tape measure

Spirit level

Disc cutter

Knee kicker

Slot-headed screwdrivers

Tenon saw

Nail punch

Chalk line

Bolster

Carpenter's pencil

Claw hammer

Panel saw

Staple punch

SELECTING FLOOR TYPES

DECORATIVE FEATURES are highly influential when it comes to choosing flooring, but practicality also has to be considered, and the ease with which a floor can be laid. Take your time when weighing up options before making choices.

COMMON FLOOR TYPES

Floor types are many and various, but most of them fall into four main categories.

- **Wooden flooring** These range from basic planking to veneers. Block floors are another option.
- **Carpets** These include good-quality hessian-backed as well as less expensive foam-backed varieties. Naturally occurring fibres such as seagrass and jute also fall into this category.
- **Utility flooring** Sheet flooring, such as vinyl and linoleum, is hardwearing and washable. Carpet and vinyl tiles are more decorative yet still practical.
- **Ceramic tiles** These make the most hardwearing floors and offer a huge decorative choice.

Ceramic floor tile

Vinyl floor tile

Vinyl sheet flooring

Parquet flooring strip

Floorboard

Parquet flooring panel

Seagrass

Carpet

Carpet tile

CONSIDERING OPTIONS

All purely decorative considerations aside, the economics of buying and laying flooring deserve serious consideration. A major factor is how long you expect a floor to last. Flooring is not permanent, but neither is it easily removed, and it represents a significant financial investment.

BUDGETING
- **Considering your stay** Many floor coverings are difficult to remove once fitted, so will have to be left behind when you move home. Bear this in mind when deciding how much to spend on flooring.
- **Including the preparation** Consider the preparation that might be required prior to laying a floor. It may prove costly to lay flooring if the subfloor requires a great deal of work. Old floorboards, for example, would need a lot of preparation to make them ready for laying ceramic tiles.

REFLECTING ON STYLE
- **Planning an entire room** Remember to include flooring when colour-scheming and styling a room. Obtain floor swatches as well as paint and paper samples. Budgeting will be far easier if you consider flooring when you plan the rest of your decorating.
- **Determining period** When choosing flooring, consider how its pattern and style will suit the historical period of your house, if appropriate, as well as the decoration in other rooms. Being accurate may require some research.

MEASURING UP

Working out floor surface area is relatively simple: just multiply together the relevant dimensions. Bear in mind a few other considerations, depending on the flooring.

- **Wooden floors** Allow ten per cent extra for wastage arising from cutting.
- **Carpets** These are sold in rolls. Work out the direction in which it will be unrolled to minimize wastage.
- **Tiles** Allow extra tiles for any cutting that will be required at joins and edges.

CONSIDERING PRACTICALITIES

The suitablility of a flooring for a particular room is determined by the function of that room, how much flooring is required, and your preference. Any floor covering is clearly better suited to some areas than others, depending on its comfort, appearance, and durability.

SELECTING SUITABLE FLOORING FOR EACH INDIVIDUAL ROOM

Carpet is most suitable for a bedroom, providing comfort and a soft surface to walk on

Flooring need not be as hardwearing on a landing as in a hallway, since there is less traffic and some of it may be barefoot

Vinyl tiles are excellent for tolerating water splashes in a bathroom

Natural-fibre coverings such as seagrass or jute are hardwearing and practical for a living room

Rugs add colour and comfort

Any wooden flooring is suitable for a hallway, since it will be hardwearing, easily cleaned, and able to tolerate large amounts of traffic

Vinyl flooring or linoleum is totally sealed and easily wiped clean of kitchen spillages and grease spots

Choosing flooring to suit function

When choosing flooring for a particular room in a home, it is essential to bear in mind how much the area will be used and whether, for example, people using the room will be wearing outdoor shoes or going barefoot. There are many options to choose from for each room in the home.

CONSIDERING OCCUPANTS

● **Children** Luxury carpeting can easily be spoiled by the activities of children. Consider laying inexpensive carpet or another type of flooring while children are young.

● **Pets** Hard flooring may be advisable in rooms to which animals have access. Young cats and dogs can spoil carpet and natural-fibre flooring.

CHOOSING MATERIALS

● **Establishing fibre content** Make sure that no-one is allergic to the constituent materials of a floor covering. You cannot afford to discover this after you have fitted it.

● **Going for quality** Choose as good a quality of flooring as you can afford. The better the quality, the longer the flooring will last without looking worn.

DISGUISING PROBLEMS

● **Protecting corridors** The flooring in areas leading into adjoining rooms usually wears most quickly. Lay hardwearing flooring, or protect these areas by also laying rugs or carpets.

● **Adjusting to lifestyle** In busy households, choose a patterned or flecked carpet to disguise wear. Stains and dirt will also be camouflaged.

PREPARING FLOORS

BEFORE NEW FLOORING CAN BE LAID, an existing floor may require renovation so that it is in a good enough condition to accept a new covering. As with all decorating, sound preparation is most likely to produce the best finished product.

REPAIRING FLOORBOARDS

Floorboards deteriorate over time and may need repairing in order to bring them up to a satisfactory standard. Sometimes this will require total board replacement, but most of the problems resulting from normal wear and tear can be solved with far less drastic action.

PATCHING PROBLEM AREAS

● **Replacing sections** Remove an area of defective boards using a tenon saw. Cut through the boards at the nearest joist to either side. Saw board edges at a 45-degree angle to make the replacement section slightly less obvious.
● **Patching tongue and groove** To remove a damaged section of tongue and groove, saw down each length of board, as well as at each end, in order to cut through the interlocking device. Use a hacksaw to cut through any hidden nails.
● **Concealing marks** To hide a badly pitted or grooved board, lift it out and turn it over so that the underside faces up.

FILLING GAPS

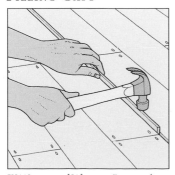

Fitting a slither of wood
Where a gap has opened up between floorboards, gently knock in a thin, wedge-shaped slither of wood with a hammer. Plane the wood down until it is flush with the floorboards.

LIFTING FLOORBOARDS

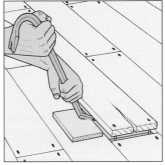

Using a crowbar
Use a crowbar to remove a floorboard quickly. Loosen any slightly protruding nails with the curled end of the crowbar. Then pivot it on a block of wood – to avoid damaging adjacent boards – as you lever out the board.

MAKING MINOR REPAIRS

● **Fixing warped boards** Use screws rather than nails to hold down bulging boards, since the thread of a screw will pull a board down and prevent it from bouncing up (which happens with nails). Remember to counter-sink the screws to keep a level surface.
● **Filling minor cracks** Fill small cracks with all-purpose filler. If the floor will be exposed, mix in a little wood dye with the filler to match the colour of the floorboards.
● **Silencing creaks** Sprinkle talcum powder in the gaps between creaking boards. This should lessen the noise.

SAFETY

When replacing floorboards, think about all the safety aspects of the job.

● **Locating pipes** Pipes and cables are often hidden beneath floors. Always proceed with caution near these potential hazards if you are repairing a floor. Use a pipe and cable detector to find them, then indicate their positions with chalk marks.
● **Avoiding nails** When working with floorboards, beware of protruding nails. When you have removed a board, be careful where you put it because nails on the underside might cause injury.

BRIGHT IDEA

Matching existing colour
Use a good board from an inconspicuous area, such as under a rug, to replace a damaged or discoloured board that is visible. Put a new one under the rug instead.

PREPARING SUBFLOORS

If a floor – whether it consists of a concrete screed or is floorboarded – is to be covered, the surface will need the appropriate preparation depending on the type of floor covering to be fitted. As a general rule, floorboards will need covering and concrete will require levelling.

MAKING A START

● **Removing lumps of concrete** Lumps of mortar can be hard to see. To locate them, slide a batten across the floor flush to the surface. Protrusions will impede the batten's progress. Remove them with a lump hammer and bolster chisel.

● **Filling gaps** Fill small holes with exterior filler or a general cement mix. To correct an undulating floor, pour over a mix of self-levelling compound.

● **Soaking hardboard** Brush water over hardboard lengths, and leave them in the room in which they are to be used for 48 hours. This allows them to acclimatize to the room, preventing edge expansion or contraction once they are laid.

● **Arranging hardboard** Lay lengths of hardboard in a brick-bond pattern, so that seams are continuous in one direction only. Make sure, too, that the seams do not coincide with floorboard joints below.

REDUCING DUST

● **Sealing concrete** Concrete floors are always dusty, so before laying carpets seal the floor with a solution of five parts water to one part PVA. Apply easily with a large pasting brush or a soft broom.

STRENGTHENING BOARDS

● **Inserting a nog** Having removed a damaged board, insert a nog, or small block of wood, between the floor joists as a support before fitting a new board. Make sure that the nog is flush with the joist tops.

REMOVING OLD FLOOR COVERINGS

It is best to remove all traces of an existing floor covering before you prepare for a new one.

● **Carpet** Discard old carpets but keep the gripper rods, since they can be reused. Underlay may also be used again.
● **Vinyl flooring** Depending on how much adhesive was used to fix it, vinyl will usually lift fairly easily. A hot-air gun will soften vinyl and speed up its removal. Take care when using a hot-air gun (see p. 74).
● **Ceramic tiles** As long as they are level, ceramic tiles make a good base for a new floor, and should be left undisturbed.

Removing floor tiles
Floor tiles or linoleum or can become brittle with age, and the strong adhesive used to attach them makes their removal difficult. Slide a spade beneath them, and break sections away.

CUTTING TO FIT AND ATTACHING A HARDBOARD SUBFLOOR

1 If part of a hardboard sheet is required, cut it to fit in position. Place it rough-side up, butting up to any skirting. Mark with a pencil the points on each edge where it reaches the sheets that have been laid.

2 Join the two marks using a straight edge, and cut along the line with a craft knife, using a steel rule to keep the cut straight. Score deeply into the board, and bend it along the line. It should break cleanly.

3 Lay the hardboard in place smooth-side-up. Staple it down using a staple gun, which is inexpensive to hire and quick to use. This laying method ensures that only perimeter edges are not factory-finished.

LAYING WOODEN FLOORS

W OOD DEMONSTRATES GREAT VERSATILITY when used for flooring. It makes an excellent subfloor on which to lay other floor coverings, and it can be laid in a number of different ways to produce an attractive finish in its own right.

RENOVATING OLD FLOORS

L aying a new wooden floor can sometimes be avoided by renovating an existing one and giving it a decorative finish. There are obvious financial advantages to this approach since the raw material is already there, and a simple process is all that is required to finish it off.

MAKING DECISIONS
● **Considering amount of use** If a floor needs a lot of repair or board replacement (see p. 90), decide whether or not the renovation is worthwhile. This will depend on how much you use the room.
● **Covering a floor** If you are covering a floor with rugs so that only a small part is visible, the wooden surface will not be a prominent feature, and need not be highly finished.
● **Assessing the job** When planning floor renovation, assess the work required to finish it. A rustic, distressed look will take far less work than a highly polished finish.

USING STRIPPER
● **Considering floor size** Use chemical stripper on a small floor, or when only a small proportion of a floor requires stripping. Chemical stripper is not economical when it is used for large areas.
● **Masking** Use at least 5-cm (2-in) masking tape along the lower edge of skirting to prevent stripping solution from reaching its painted surface.
● **Putting on and taking off** Dab on stripper with an old paintbrush, working in 50-cm (1½-ft) squares. Once it reacts, scrape away paint or varnish with a broad-bladed scraper or a wire brush on uneven floors.

BRIGHT IDEA

Masking a door
If a large floor area requires sanding, mask around the door's edges to prevent dust from escaping. Open windows to allow dust to drift outside.

USING AN INDUSTRIAL FLOOR SANDER

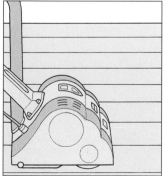

1 Start the sander in a slightly tilted back position, lower it to the surface, and proceed diagonally across the wood grain to smooth any rough areas. Use medium-grade sandpaper during this stage.

2 Change to a finer grade of paper, and sand with the grain this time. The number of times you have to do this will depend on the condition of the floorboards. Three or four times is usually sufficient.

SANDING EFFICIENTLY
● **Protecting yourself** Always wear goggles and a mask to protect yourself from flying particles and dust inhalation.
● **Removing protrusions** Use a hammer and nail punch to knock in protruding nails, otherwise the sandpaper will tear, and there is a risk that you will damage the sander.
● **Dealing with edges** Most industrial sanders will not reach right to the edge of a floor, so use a hand-held electric sander to finish off.
● **Reaching corners** Wrap some sandpaper around the end of a screwdriver to get right into corners. This will create a neat, squared finish.

LAYING NEW FLOORS

There are several ways of laying a new wooden floor. This is because there are several different construction systems that can be adapted to go over most existing subfloors. Follow the manufacturer's specific instructions when dealing with proprietary products.

PREPARING TO LAY

● **Checking levels** Ensure that all joists are level by laying a long length of batten across them. Check that the underside of the batten is touching the top of the joists all along its length. Any gaps should be filled with slithers of wood.

● **Ensuring dryness** Make sure that a new concrete screed is completely dry before you lay a wooden floor, otherwise damp from the subfloor will cause the wood to buckle. Check newly laid screeds with a damp-detector gauge.

● **Acclimatizing wood** Store wooden flooring in the room in which it is to be laid for at least 48 hours before it is used. This will allow it to expand or contract slightly as it adjusts to the room temperature.

DESIGNING A LAYOUT

You have several options when it comes to designing the layout of a planked or tongue-and-groove floor. Much will depend on your woodworking skills.

● **Parallel** This is the most straightforward design and requires a minimal amount of technical know-how.
● **Diagonal** This design requires good planning and accurate woodwork, especially if you are laying directly on top of joists.
● **Concentric** A concentric, square or rectangular design requires an appropriately shaped room and a solid wooden or floating subfloor. If planks are to run in two directions, as in this design, a joisted subfloor will not have enough surface area in which to secure nails.

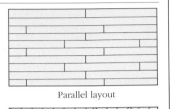

Parallel layout

Diagonal layout

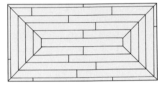

Concentric layout

TONGUE-AND-GROOVING

● **Avoiding adjacent joins** Stagger ends of boards so that cut ends of adjacent planks do not coincide. Nail ends down, or use secret nailing (see p. 55).

Butting up
Make sure that lengths of tongue and groove are butted up tightly. To protect a board that is being fitted from damage, use a small offcut of board as a driving tool against which to hammer.

DEALING WITH EDGES

● **Hiding gaps** Cover gaps between skirting and floor with strips of moulding of either a quadrant (convex) or a scotia (concave) variety.

Fixing moulding
Attach moulding to a skirting board rather than to the floor to allow for floor movement, which might pull the moulding away. Use oval-headed nails, which need minimal filling once knocked in.

CONSIDERING OPTIONS

● **Using underlay** You can lay some floors on to polyfoam underlay rather than wooden joists or frames. These are "floating" floors, since they have no solid fixing and rely on jointing mechanisms to ensure stability. Fix skirting after laying the floor, so as to cover the gap left around the edge of the floor to allow for expansion.
● **Fixing with clips** Hide floor fixings by using metal clips, which will hold floorboards together without being visible. Insert the clips beneath and along the floorboard joins.
● **Buying pre-finished flooring** You may choose a floor that requires no finishing once it is laid. It will be more expensive and require care when laying, but you will save a lot of time and money in the long term.

LAYING WOOD-BLOCK FLOORS

Traditionally, wood-block floors were literally made up of rectangular wooden blocks, laid tightly butted up against each other in a variety of patterns. Wood-block floors are now made in strips or panels of rectangles, which are less costly to produce but create the same effect.

PREPARING FLOORS

● **Choosing a subfloor** Blocks and panels require a very flat surface. Concrete screeds are ideal, while hardboard and chipboard are suitable as long as you make sure that there is no flexibility in movement as you walk across them.

● **Starting in the middle** Find the centre of a room using a chalkline (see p. 99), thus dividing the floor into four. Complete one section before moving on to the next.

● **Cleaning surfaces** Vacuum clean the floor and wash it with a mop before starting to lay blocks or panels. This will remove dust and grit particles which might prevent the floor from being laid dead level.

ALLOWING FOR MOVEMENT

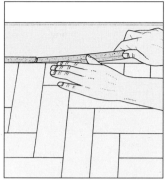

Coping with expansion

Leave a 1-cm ($\frac{3}{8}$-in) gap around the perimeter of a wood-block or panel floor to allow for expansion caused by changing humidity. Infill with cork strips to prevent edges from buckling or lifting, and to improve the finish.

FITTING PANELS

● **Applying adhesive** Flooring adhesive tends to be very viscous. Apply it with a grout spreader and work in areas no larger than 1 m² (1 sq yd).

● **Tapping into place** Panels will require "bedding in". Tap each one down by gently hammering a block of wood placed on top of it. This will avoid damaging the panel surface, and will apply a more even pressure across it.

● **Dealing with obstacles** Panels consist of equally sized wooden "fingers". Before you lay a floor, split a couple into sections ranging from groups of three to single fingers. You will thus have a choice of sizes for trimming around obstacles.

SEALING FLOORS

Most wooden floors need to have some sort of finish before they are used, to protect them from wear and tear. The choice of products varies from traditional waxes that require regular maintenance to hardwearing varnishes that provide the toughest finish of all.

VARNISHING EVENLY

Keeping to edges

Apply a coloured finish to a planked floor one floorboard at a time, otherwise overlapping brush strokes will produce different levels of colour intensity and a patchy finish.

COVERING EFFICIENTLY

● **Sealing with varnish** Thin the first coat of varnish slightly. It will then act as a primer, soaking in well and sealing the wooden surface.

● **Using quick-drying varnishes** Use acrylic or water-based varnishes, since more than one coat can be applied in a day. This means that you will be able to get the floor back in use as quickly as possible.

● **Protecting high-wear areas** Apply extra coats of varnish to door entrances and natural "corridors" within a room. Use a clear varnish, otherwise there will be too great a build-up of colour in those areas that are receiving extra coats.

MONEY-SAVING TIP

Polishing waxed floors
To buff up a waxed surface, attach a soft cloth to the end of a broom. (After the first application of wax to a newly laid floor, you might like to hire a polisher for buffing up.)

CARPETING FLOORS

Carpet laying is a job that is often left to professional carpet fitters, but there is no reason why you cannot do it as long as you follow the manufacturer's instructions. Carpet materials vary and, consequently, so do laying techniques.

LAYING HESSIAN-BACKED CARPET

Hessian-backed carpet is among the very best in terms of quality. The strong hessian backing always provides excellent durability. The type of pile, fibre, and weave can vary among hessian-backed carpets, but the laying techniques remain more or less constant.

SECURING CURVED EDGES

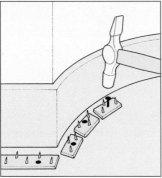

Using gripper rods
Gripper rods are straight and rigid, so saw them into 5-cm (2-in) sections to round a curved area such as a bay window. Attach them to the floor close to the skirting board in the usual way.

LEARNING THE BASICS
● **Using underlay** Always use a good-quality underlay below hessian-backed carpet. Felt or rubber varieties are suitable and provide extra comfort as well as increasing the life of the carpet. Do not lay underlay over the gripper rods.
● **Cutting roughly** Roll out a carpet, and cut it roughly to size. Allow an additional 15 cm (6 in) around the perimeter for final trimming.
● **Joining carpet** Not all rooms are regularly shaped, and you may have to join carpet rolls before fitting them. Obtain professional help with this. Most suppliers will join lengths so that seams are invisible.

TRADITIONAL TIP

Tacking carpet
When fixing carpet in position, a less expensive alternative to using gripper rods is to nail down carpet edges with tacks. Fold the edges of the carpet over, and nail through the folds.

LAYING FOAM-BACKED CARPET

Foam-backed carpet is usually less expensive and easier to lay than hessian-backed carpet.

● **Preparing** Underlay is not usually required, but cover the floor with newspaper before laying the carpet to reduce dust and abrasion between carpet backing and floor.
● **Fixing** Foam-backed carpet is relatively lightweight, so attach it to the floor with double-sided carpet tape.
● **Joining** Use single-sided tape to join lengths of carpet from below, ensuring that the pile goes in the same direction.

TRIMMING CARPET

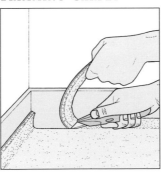

Using a craft knife
Trim hessian-backed carpet tightly up to the skirting board using a craft knife. Keep the cut straight, although imperfections will be hidden when you stretch the carpet over the gripper rods.

FITTING CARPET

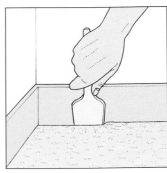

Using a bolster
Having stretched and smoothed out the carpet to the gripper rods with a knee kicker, use a bolster to push the carpet firmly over and behind the gripper rods at the skirting–floor junction.

LAYING NATURAL-FIBRE FLOORING

Natural-fibre flooring such as sisal is both decorative and hardwearing. The types of fibre used vary, but this causes only subtle variations in the pattern, texture, and comfort that they offer. Laying techniques differ only slightly from the methods used to lay carpet.

CARING FOR FLOORING

● **Acclimatizing** Allow a natural floor covering to acclimatize in the room in which it is to be laid for at least 24 hours before fitting. It will need to adjust to the room's humidity.

● **Prolonging life** Check in the manufacturer's guidelines, but a natural floor covering such as rush can benefit from the occasional light watering. A household plant sprayer is ideal to use for this purpose.

● **Using underlay** Attach underlay to natural-fibre flooring using proprietary adhesive. This will have the effect of smoothing an uneven subfloor as well as providing extra comfort underfoot. Underlay is not necessary with natural floor coverings that already have a latex backing.

USING DECORATIVE RUGS

Rugs, in a wide variety of designs, are traditional floor-decorating accessories. They can be used to complement other floor coverings, or enhance a plain floor by adding a splash of colour. Small decorative rugs are particularly useful for both adding colour and providing extra comfort when laid upon natural-fibre floor coverings.

● **Choosing rugs** The choice includes bold ethnic rugs such as kilims and durries – usually cotton or wool; modern, synthetic, mass-produced rugs; and sophisticated traditional weaves, often from Central Asia or China. You can decide to buy an inexpensive rug, or look upon a high-quality rug as an investment, and pay a lot more.

Creating a splash of colour Rugs that incorporate many different colours in their design are often easy to fit into a colour scheme. Splashes of colour that blend or contrast with a room's colour scheme both enhance the decorative appeal of the rug itself and provide a decorative focal point within the room.

LAYING FLOORING ON STAIRS

Laying flooring on stairs presents the problem of working vertically as well as horizontally. More trimming is necessary as a result, so there is more wastage. You will also need to allow more time for laying flooring on stairs.

● **Using natural-fibre flooring** If you want to cover stairs with materials such as seagrass or jute, follow manufacturers' guidelines carefully. The rigidity and therefore the ability of these materials to fit stair profiles varies, making the use of different fixing methods necessary.

● **Fixing hessian-backed carpet** Attach an appropriate length of gripper rod to the bottom of each riser and at the back of each tread to make sure that the carpet is secured as firmly as possible on each stair.

● **Laying foam-backed carpet** Staple along the back of each tread to attach foam-backed carpet to stairs. This will fix it in place and stop it from slipping.

● **Starting at the top** When fitting stair carpet, place the first fixing firmly on the landing before continuing downstairs.

● **Placing stair rods** Fit a stair rod at the tread–riser junction to reduce the possibility of the carpet slipping. The rods can be painted to match the colour of the carpet before you fit them to make them less conspicuous.

● **Reversing carpet** Before a stair carpet begins to wear in places – and if the dimensions of the treads and risers are the same – take up the carpet and reverse it top to bottom to extend its life. The treads will become risers and vice versa.

Finishing off at the bottom Trim the end of a length of stair carpet so that it folds under the lip of the bottom tread. Cut a jagged edge, allowing the carpet to mould around the curved edge. Fix with tacks or a staple gun. Fit a final piece of carpet over the jagged edge.

LAYING UTILITY FLOORING

Some areas of the home demand flooring that is both easy to clean and very durable. Once thought of purely in practical terms, most utility flooring is now cushioned for comfort, and a large range of designs give it scope decoratively.

SHEET FLOORING

There are three catgories of sheet flooring: vinyl, linoleum, and rubber. Vinyl is very versatile, being available in a range of thicknesses and other properties. Rubber and linoleum are less common but are still in demand for their specific properties and characteristic finishes.

LAYING SHEET FLOORING
● **Preparing a subfloor** Clean a subfloor thoroughly – whether it is concrete or hardboard – to make sure that there are no traces of dirt or grit, or lumps of any kind. Imperfections such as these can push into the back of the flooring, causing a weak spot that will eventually wear through.
● **Choosing adhesive** Flooring adhesives vary considerably. Make sure that you have the correct one for your flooring.
● **Applying adhesive** Apply adhesive around the edges of a room and along any joins. Do not waste adhesive, and therefore money, by covering the whole floor with it.

MAKING AN ACCURATE TEMPLATE FOR CUTTING

1 Cover the subfloor with sheets of newspaper, fitting them exactly around the edges of any obstacles. Tape all the pieces together, creating a large template that is the exact size and shape of the floor.

2 Tape the paper template securely to the flooring. Work in a large enough space to be able to lay the template completely flat. Cut the flooring around the template so that it will fit the floor.

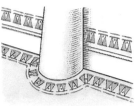

BRIGHT IDEA

Designing linoleum
Many manufacturers will make linoleum flooring to your requirements. You can design your own pattern, picking up a detail in a wallpaper, for example.

NEATENING EDGES
● **Cutting precisely** Push the edge of vinyl or other sheet flooring into the floor–skirting junction with a broad-bladed scraper. Cut precisely along the crease guideline with a sharp craft knife. Disguise imperfections with moulding.
● **Reducing cutting** Remove kicker boards in kitchens and bath panels in bathrooms, and lay flooring underneath these fittings. Replace the boards or panels to give a precise edge.
● **Waterproofing** Run a thin bead of clear silicone around flooring and skirting edges to make the surface completely waterproof and easy to clean.

JOINING SHEETS

Making a butt join
Join two sheets of flooring as you would wallpaper. Overlap the edges and, using a steel-rule guideline, cut through both sheets. Remove excess pieces and stick down the edges of the vinyl.

SOFT-TILE FLOORING

Many of the recommendations and methods applicable to sheet flooring also apply to soft-tile flooring, since tiles are made from the same materials. Other types of soft-tile flooring include cork and carpet tiles, and the same rules apply to application and fitting of these.

PLANNING THE JOB
● **Protecting a floor** Do not walk on a newly tiled surface for at least 24 hours while the adhesive dries. Tile in two halves, so that one part can be used while the other dries.

APPLYING ADHESIVE
● **Spreading evenly** Apply tile adhesive using a notched spreader. Cover about four tiles at once – a convenient working area – so that the adhesive does not dry too quickly.

FLATTENING TILES
● **Rollering down** Tiles will usually flatten and stick down easily. To ensure an absolutely flat surface, gently roll over the tiles with a rolling pin just after they have been laid.

FINDING THE CENTRE

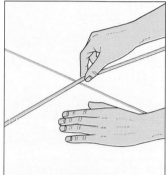

Snapping a guideline
To locate the centre of a room, snap a chalk line (see p. 34) between the mid-points of opposite walls. Use the chalk lines as guides for laying the first row of tiles in each quadrant.

CUTTING TILES TO FIT AROUND A CORNER

1 Lay the tile to be cut exactly on top of the nearest whole tile to the corner. Lay another tile on top of this, but with its edge butting right up to the skirting. Draw a line along its edge on the tile to be cut.

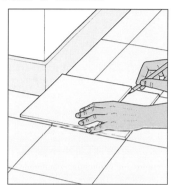

2 Without rotating the tile to be cut, move both tiles around the corner to the nearest whole tile, and repeat the process. The lines you have drawn will show where to cut the tile to fit the corner.

TILING CLEVERLY
● **Cleaning off adhesive** Adhesive often gets on to tile surfaces. Keep white spirit and a cloth handy so that you can remove it immediately. Some manufacturers may suggest alternative solvents for this.
● **Making templates** Cut some pieces of paper exactly to tile size before you begin. Use them to make templates of awkward areas such as those around the bases of door architraves.
● **Negotiating pipes** Fitting a template around a pipe is not easy. Mark the pipe's position on a tile, then use a pipe offcut to create an accurate impression on the tile itself.

LAYING CARPET TILES

Carpet tiles are a practical, all-purpose flooring. They are more comfortable than vinyl tiles and easier to clean than carpet itself. Stained tiles can be replaced.

● **Sticking carpet tiles** Lay carpet tiles in the same way as soft tiles, except that there is no need to fix them, apart from around door thresholds, where double-sided tape can be used.
● **Butting up** Cut some plywood to the size of a tile. Stick a piece of batten to the centre of one side as a handle. Attach four or five cut lengths of gripper rod to the other side. Use this to pick up and butt up tiles tightly.

Place shape in cut-out

Creating footprints
Cut left and right foot shapes out of different-coloured floor tiles from the main colour. Cut the exact same shape out of a few of the main-colour tiles and infill with the cut-out "feet". Position the tiles so that the footprints lead across the room.

LAYING HARD-TILE FLOORING

FLOOR TILES ARE USUALLY LARGER and more substantial than wall tiles because they are load bearing and need to be more robust. There is a large variety of hard tiles from which to choose to complement other decoration in a room.

DESIGNS AND TECHNIQUES

Laying floor tiles is similar to attaching wall tiles, and many of the same principles and techniques apply. Mistakes in laying floors can prove expensive to rectify, so always make sure that you plan the job very carefully before you start work, and follow the instructions.

LAYING QUARRY TILES

● **Planning a layout** When working out exactly where floor tiles are to be positioned, use a tile gauge (see p. 62).

● **Starting out** In rooms with straight and true walls, use the skirting boards as guidelines. This should reduce the amount of cutting necessary on at least two walls. If the walls are not true, start tiling from battened edges. Leave a gap between battens and walls so that infill tiles used to finish off the floor will be at least half-sized.

● **Using mortar** Always lay quarry tiles in a thick bed of mortar, rather than applying ceramic tile adhesive.

DESIGNING LAYOUTS

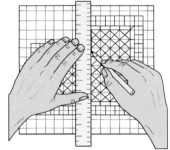

Planning a design
For an intricately patterned floor, make a plan to scale of where each tile will be positioned. This is especially important when you are intending to use marble inset tiles, to ensure that each one is laid in exactly the right place.

SPACING FLOOR TILES

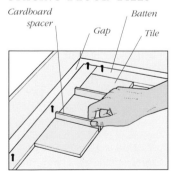

Cardboard spacer

Batten

Gap

Tile

Maintaining gaps
Floor tiles rarely have spacing mechanisms built into their design, so wedge pieces of thick cardboard between the tiles to keep them apart. Remove these improvised tile spacers once the mortar has started to set.

KEEPING TILES LEVEL

Levelled mortar

Gap

Batten

Depth gauge

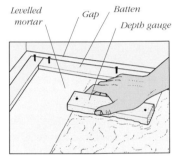

Using a depth gauge
Hammer a nail through each end of a short length of batten so that the nails protrude by 1 cm ($\frac{1}{2}$ in). Run this tool over the mortar, with the nails reaching through to the floor, so the mortar will be consistently 1 cm ($\frac{1}{2}$ in) thick.

TILING SKIRTING BOARDS

● **Cleaning easily** Attach a line of quarry tiles along the base of a wall as a substitute for skirting board. You will then be able to clean easily, with no gap between floor and wall.

SAFETY

If you hire a disc cutter to speed up floor-tiling, follow these safety precautions.

● **Following instructions** Always read manufacturers' guidelines about operating disc cutters safely.
● **Protecting yourself** Wear a dust mask and goggles to protect the eyes from splinters.

TIME-SAVING TIP

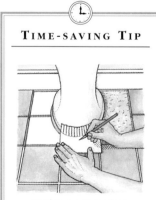

Making a template
Most floor coverings need a few fiddly cuts. Make templates around all obstacles, and let your local supplier make all your floor-tile cuts for you.

CERAMIC TILES

Much of the methodology for laying hard floor tiles can also be applied to ceramic floor tiles. However, with ceramic tiles you will have a little more flexibility when it comes to laying techniques. Since they are less heavy-duty, ceramic tiles are easier to work with.

MAKING ADJUSTMENTS

● **Dealing with doors** Remove doors that open on to a tiled floor surface before laying the tiles. Shave the same amount off the bottom of the door as the depth of a tile plus a little extra to allow for adhesive.

● **Finishing off the threshold** Cut a strip of hardwood doorstop the same width as the door to create an excellent threshold strip that is both decorative and provides a good barrier against which to tile.

● **Keeping level** Check that tiles are level from time to time by running a spirit level or batten over the surface of newly laid tiles. Make any necessary adjustments while the adhesive is still wet, since mistakes will be difficult to rectify once it has dried.

● **Using inserts** To give a tiled area an opulent feel without spending a lot of money, buy a few high-quality, patterned tiles, and design a panel to insert in an appropriate place to lift the floor's appearance.

MAKING MOSAIC PANELS

● **Using an MDF base** When creating a mosaic panel as an insert feature to enhance a plain floor, attach the mosiac tiles to a piece of MDF cut to measure. The MDF will provide a rigid, sturdy base.

CUTTING SMALL PIECES

● **Using a nibbler** As with wall tiles, when you have to cut intricate shapes – or if you want to cut up pieces of tile for insertion in a mosaic – use a nibbler to give you greater accuracy (see p. 64).

INLAYING MOSAICS WITHIN TILED FLOORS

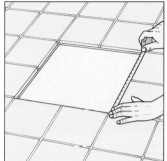

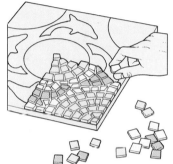

1 Leave a hole the size of the area required by the mosaic design within the floor layout. Cut a piece of MDF to fit the hole, making sure that it is of the correct thickness so that, once tiled and inlaid, the mosaic will be level with the surrounding tiled surface.

2 Draw the design you want on the MDF, and infill with mosaic tiles. Make sure that you use floor adhesive to fix them in place, as this is the strongest method. Once complete, fit the mosaic into its hole. Use floor adhesive to fix the MDF base in position.

CREATING A RUSTIC LOOK

As well as tiles that are custom- or factory-made, there are other alternatives that you can use for decorative hard flooring. These include a variety of more natural-looking materials. The particular characteristics of these products mean that you should consider practical requirements carefully.

● **Flagstones** These are extremely heavy-duty and can be found in regular or irregular shapes. Their surfaces tend to be uneven, so it is essential that you bed them in with plenty of mortar.

● **Bricks** These are best laid on their sides, especially if you want to create a herringbone pattern. Bricks should be bedded in mortar and butted up tightly together. Once laid, cover with as many coats of varnish or proprietary floor sealer as possible to seal the surface.

● **Slate** Make sure that the subfloor is perfectly level before using slate tiles. Lay them on to adhesive, taking great care to prevent it from getting on the upper surfaces of the tiles, since it may stain them permanently.

Moving a heavy slab
Move a heavy stone slab using a simple yet effective method. Manoeuvre the slab on to two poles, and push the slab along as if it were on wheels. Bring each pole to the front as it is left behind as the slab progresses.

PAINTING FLOORS

CONCRETE SCREEDS AND WOODEN SUBFLOORS can be painted rather than covered with flooring. Proprietary floor paints should be used in high-wear areas, but other paints are acceptable on less well-used floors, as long as you varnish them well.

CREATING WOOD EFFECTS

One of the advantages of creating a wood effect is that it is far less expensive than laying a wooden floor. Using colour cleverly, you can imitate natural wood convincingly. Alternatively, if you choose vivid colours you can create an altogether surreal finish.

PREPARING TO PAINT
● **Checking** Read manufacturers' guidelines before painting sheet flooring (hardboard and chipboard). Some sheets are impregnated with fire-retardant chemicals that render them unsuitable for painting.
● **Filling** Fill imperfections on the surface of sheet flooring with all-purpose filler, which can be sanded back to a smooth finish. Fill small gaps between sheets with flexible filler, so that the cracks will not reopen when walked on.
● **Painting** Use a roller rather than a brush to paint a floor quickly. Attach an extension pole to the roller so that you can paint standing up.

PAINTING A *FAUX* RUG

Wooden surfaces can offer an ideal opportunity for *trompe l'oeil* effects, and a *faux* rug can be particularly eye-catching. The edges of floorboards provide ready-made guidelines for painting bands of colour.

● **Planning a design** Work out a complete design for the *faux* rug before you start painting. Decide where on the floor you want the "rug" to be, and measure out an area guideline.
● **Painting narrow stripes** Use a mini roller for painting any narrow coloured stripes.
● **Increasing realism** Add fine detail freehand to increase the realism, or "cheat" with stencils.

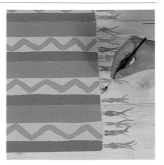

Adding the tassels
Use an artist's brush to finish off a *faux* rug by painting tassels at each end. In reality, rug tassels are often pale in colour or off-white, but use vibrant colours to show up better against wood.

CREATING THE IMPRESSION OF PAINTED FLOORBOARDS

1 Base-coat the floor, then draw pencil guidelines to represent the floorboard edges. Use an old plank or floorboard as a template which will automatically give you "boards" of the right size.

2 Mix up a glaze (see p. 31). Using the plank as a straight edge, apply a coat of glaze to each "floorboard". Draw a rocker through the glaze. Create knots by agitating the rocker backwards and forwards.

3 Once the glaze is dry, go over the pencil guidelines with a dark felt-tip pen. This will outline each "floorboard". Finally, cover the whole floor with two or three protective coats of acrylic matt varnish.

CREATING TILE EFFECTS

As in the case of wood effects, painting *faux* tiles rather than covering a floor with the real thing will greatly reduce your decorating expenditure. Tile effects are ideally suited to concrete screeds: extra realism is provided by the noise created by walking on the surface.

CREATING "HARD TILES"

● **Ensuring dryness** Make sure that a floor has totally dried out before you paint it. A new concrete screed should not be painted for several months.

● **Sealing a floor** Dilute proprietary floor paints slightly for the first coat in order to prime and seal a floor surface. If you use alternative types of paint, make sure that you coat the floor with a proprietary sealer before you start.

● **Choosing a base colour** Choose a light colour for the first coat. This will not only provide a realistic grout colour, but will also make a good foundation for the subsequent tile colours that you choose.

● **Applying paint effects** Marbling and sponging are two paint-effect techniques that lend themselves very well to creating an impression of hard-tile flooring.

CREATING THE IMPRESSION OF TERRACOTTA TILES

● **"Tiling" freehand** Painting a tile effect need not be an exact science. To avoid the need for pencil guidelines, use a square object to produce the tiles by means of block printing.

1 Use a roller tray as a paint reservoir. Load a sponge with paint, removing excess. Place the sponge firmly on the floor, and apply pressure to print a well-defined tile shape. Leave gaps to represent grout.

● **Using a sponge** Make a block for creating "tiles" from a household sponge. Most are rectangular, so cut one down to tile size. Use the trimmed pieces for filling in detail.

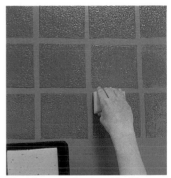

2 After producing 10–20 "tiles", apply more paint to each one with a small piece of sponge to increase opacity. This build-up of depth will help to make the tiles look textured and more realistic.

FAKING CHEQUERED VINYL TILES

1 Apply a base coat to a floor, and let it dry. Measure out and draw a chequered pattern with a pencil. Cover alternate squares with pieces of newspaper. Spray black paint over the exposed squares.

2 Once the black paint has dried, peel away the newspaper masks to reveal a chequered, fake vinyl-tiled floor. As with all paint-effect floors, apply a protective coat of varnish to finish off.

BRIGHT IDEA

Chequering wood
Create a chequered effect on floorboards with wood stain. Use floorboard edges and masking tape to define the squares. Brush wood stain on alternate squares, which will highlight the wood grain and increase the contrast.

FINISHING OFF

LAYING MANY TYPES OF FLOORING is quite a costly business, and one that you do not want to repeat very often. Make sure that the job is done well so that you reap the maximum benefit from the new floor, and it lasts as long as possible.

PROTECTING AND MAINTAINING FLOORS

A new floor covering will last a long time if it is well looked after. There are many varieties of flooring and a number of different ways of protecting and maintaining them, all of which are aimed at increasing the life of a floor and keeping it looking as good as possible.

CARING FOR CARPET
● **Cleaning** Vacuum clean carpets at least once a week, and have them professionally cleaned once a year to keep them in good condition and make them longer-lasting.
● **Protecting** In main walking thoroughfares, lay rugs on top of carpets to reduce heavy wear on the carpets. Rearrange the positions of the rugs from time to time, so that they wear more evenly and last longer.
● **Using mats** Place a mat on the floor just inside each external door. Offcuts of natural-fibre floor coverings make excellent mats, being both functional and decorative.

Using lids as coasters
Paint jam-jar lids to match the colour of a carpet. Lift heavy items of furniture, and place the lids under the feet. The larger the lid, the greater the weight distribution and the less wear on the carpet.

DISTRIBUTING WEIGHT

MAINTAINING TILES
● **Cleaning vinyl** Always remove dirt and grit with a vacuum cleaner before mopping a vinyl floor. Otherwise, the mop may push bits of grit around the floor and scratch the surface of the vinyl.
● **Washing hard tiles** Mop a hard-tile floor with warm water regularly. Buff it up occasionally with a proprietary polish designed specifically for hard-tile floors; standard polishes will make it slippery.
● **Replacing carpet tiles** Simply lift out and replace worn or badly stained carpet tiles. This is an advantage of not having fixed them in position with adhesive.

PROTECTING WOOD
● **Varnishing** Recoat well-used areas of a wooden floor at least once a year to maintain the floor's protective layer.
● **Waxing** Wax a wooden floor occasionally in order to maintain its hardwearing properties. This will also help to build up a good depth of colour and improve the appearance of the floor.
● **Underlaying rugs** Use a rug to protect a wooden floor, and insert a piece of non-slip underlay beneath it. This will have the effect of slowing down the wear of the rug by preventing it from rubbing on the hard wooden surface.

TRADITIONAL TIP

Making a sealer
Seal porous tiles with a wax made by warming four parts boiled linseed oil with one part beeswax until they are well mixed. Leave to cool, then apply to the tiles, and buff up.

REMOVING STAINS FROM CARPET

Accidental spillages and the marking of carpets will happen from time to time. Most stains can be removed with care, fast action, and sometimes a little ingenuity.

● **Speed** Act quickly, since the success of stain removal depends upon the swift removal of the spillage.
● **Action** Dab and blot stains rather than rubbing them.
● **Dampening** Do not use too much water, since this might damage the carpet backing.
● **Prevention** Treat carpets with proprietary stain guard, following makers' instructions.

USING LEFTOVERS

Offcuts and leftovers from a flooring project can be put to a variety of practical uses in many areas of the home. However, always keep back some of the spare flooring for repairing damage, or as swatches to aid decision-making about future decorating projects.

USING CARPET OFFCUTS

● **Keeping pets comfortable** Carpet makes an excellent lining for pet beds and baskets. Simply cut and fit as required.

● **Using in cars** Car boots receive a great amount of wear and tear. Line the base of a car boot with carpet to protect the bodywork from damage and to make it much easier to clean. The piece of carpet can either be lifted out of the boot to be cleaned or vacuum cleaned in situ.

● **Lining paths** Gravel paths are notoriously difficult to keep free of weeds. Line a path with pieces of old carpet or underlay offcuts cut to size before laying gravel. This will seriously impede the growth of weeds or other stray plants.

● **Covering compost** Lay carpet over the top of a compost heap to keep in heat and therefore speed up the natural processes of decomposition.

MAKING STAMPS FOR FLOOR EFFECTS

1 Cut cork into pieces the length of the strips of a parquet floor panel. Apply PVA along the edge of each cork piece, and attach to the panel. Stick a block of wood to the back of the panel as a handle.

2 Base-coat the floor, and allow to dry. Load the stamp from a paint tray using a short-haired mohair roller. Position the stamp, and apply pressure to transfer the paint well. Reload after each impression.

USING VINYL

● **Cushioning movement** Cut up sheet vinyl or tiles, and lay beneath a washing machine. Vinyl will provide a sturdy base but cushion the vibrations.

USING HARD TILES

● **Absorbing heat** Quarry tiles are thick and sturdy, and make excellent pan rests. Use them to protect a worktop from hot pan bases removed from a hob.

USING UP CORK TILES

Cork is a versatile material, and leftovers can be put to a number of uses in the home.

● **Making coasters** Place an upturned drinking glass on a cork tile, and draw around the rim. Cut out the shape to make a coaster.

● **Catering for cats** Stick a few cork tiles on to a block of wood for your cat to use as a scratcher instead of the furniture.

● **Making pads** Cut pieces of cork tile to fit the bottoms of heavy ornaments. Stick them in position to protect the surface of furniture and prevent the ornaments from slipping.

Making a notice board
Attach some plyboard to the back of a picture frame. Use neat PVA to stick cork tiles to the front surface of the plyboard until the frame is filled. Remove excess PVA with a damp cloth. Hang the frame in the usual way and use it as a notice board.

PROTECTING DOORS

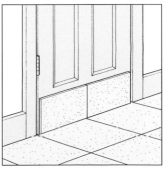

Making a kicker
The base of a door can easily be damaged by children and pets. Reduce this wear and tear by making a kicker board out of spare carpet tiles. Use spray adhesive to attach the tiles along the bottom edge of the door.

Dressing Windows

Quick Reference

Selecting Materials, p. 108

Choosing Curtains, p. 109

Choosing Blinds, p. 112

Adding Trimmings, p. 114

Decorating Glass, p. 116

Window dressings are an important part of the decorative appeal of most rooms in the home. The options range from extravagant curtains and valances to plain blinds or shutters. These are all traditional ways of decorating windows, but with a little creativity you can break loose from convention and introduce your own innovative ideas.

Looking at Windows

Before choosing any window dressing, look at the style and shape of a particular window, and consider all decorative options. Take into account the practical functions that dressings will serve, such as increasing privacy, keeping out the cold or heat, or blocking light.

Common Window Types

Window types and sizes vary considerably. Adapt your window dressings accordingly.

- **Sash** These are often tall and narrow. "Widen" them with curtains and a half-drawn blind.
- **French** Draw curtains right back from the frame to ensure easy opening and closing.
- **Picture** These are simple in design. Choose from all types of window dressing.
- **Bay** Consider carefully the hanging system required for these multi-faceted windows.
- **Casement** These vary greatly in size and design. Assess each one individually.

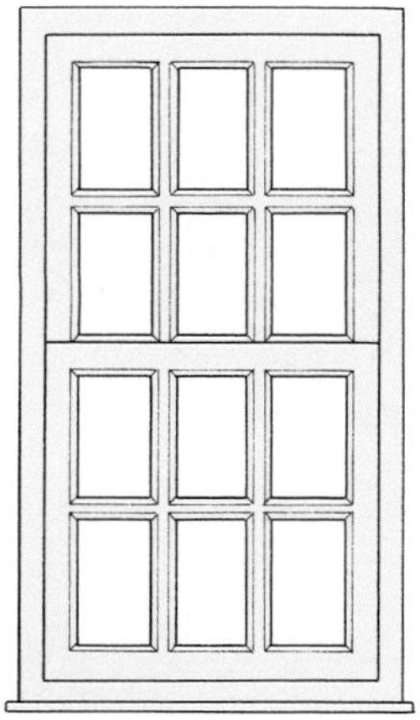

Sash window

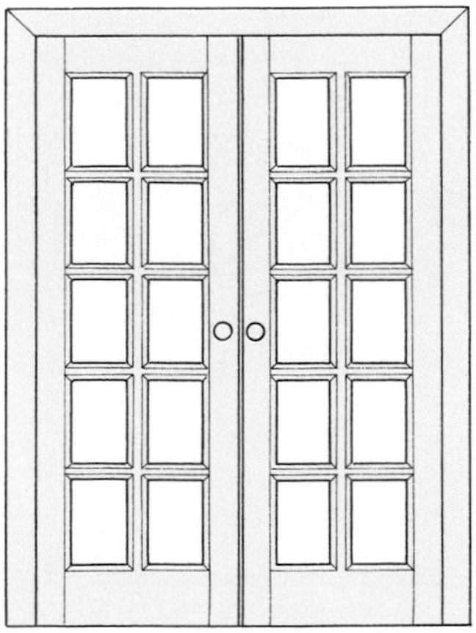

French windows

Picture window

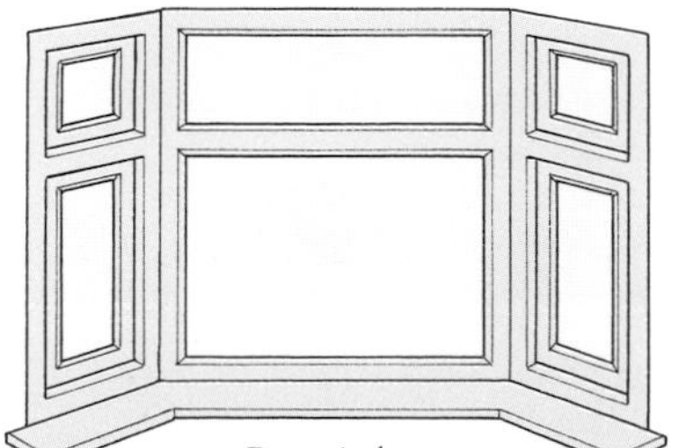

Bay window

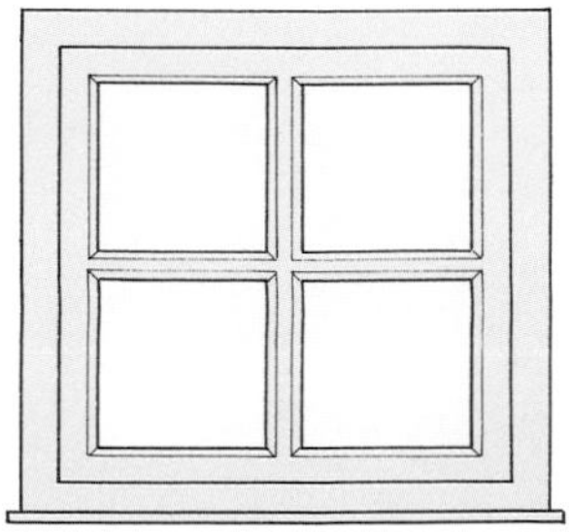

Casement window

SETTING A STYLE

Choosing window dressings can give you a wonderful opportunity to release your own artistic flair. Whether you drape lavish swathes of expensive fabric or adopt a more minimalist approach, the decorative style of a room can often be set by the window dressing alone.

CONSIDERING OPTIONS

Before choosing fabrics and styles of window dressing, think about these purely practical considerations.

● **Function** Choose simple, inexpensive hanging systems whenever you can, especially if your window dressings are purely decorative. You may need to invest in more costly hanging systems if you decide to hang curtains made of heavyweight material for warmth, for example.
● **Budget** Very full drapes usually result in great expense, so make sure that you work out what your budgetary restrictions are before you make choices.
● **Theme** If you decide to try to follow a regional or period theme, research appropriate materials, designs, and colours in order to create a complete, authentic look.

KEEPING FABRICS PLAIN
● **Colour scheming simply** Use plain materials to make colour scheming easier. Window dressings will thus play a complementary decorative role.

Dressing up plain fabric
Although a fabric may be plain in colour, drape it effectively with an unusual tie-back. Use windowsills as display areas for interesting collections of objects.

MAKING A STATEMENT
● **Drawing attention** If you want a window dressing to be a focal point, choose bold or contrasting colours and patterns to draw the eye.

Enhancing embellishments
Emphasize a flouncy window dressing by offsetting it against understated walls. Paint walls off-white or an extremely pale, complementary colour.

TREATING A WINDOW IN DIFFERENT WAYS

Disguising window shape
Curtains hung outside a recess will disguise the shape of a window, especially if tied back from a closed position. Use a shaped valance to disguise the squareness of a window.

Emphasizing window shape
Hang a blind inside a window recess to emphasize the shape of the window. A patterned blind will draw attention to clear lines and square angles, and help to make the window a feature.

SETTING THE SCENE
● **Having fun** Choose an appropriate fabric and use it for curtains, bedcovers, and cushions to produce a sense of fun in a child's room.
● **Aiding relaxation** Indulge yourself in swathes of curtain material in restful colours for a lounge that is used for calm recreation and relaxation.
● **Improving light** Use pale coloured dressings at windows that receive little or no direct sunlight. These will encourage the greatest amount of light reflection into the room.
● **Increasing privacy** In private areas of the home, such as a bedroom, cover the windows completely to help to create a secure, restful mood.

SELECTING MATERIALS

SELECTING THE RIGHT MATERIALS when dressing windows is as important as in any other decorating job. All tasks at this stage of your project will be easiest if you use the equipment and materials that are specifically designed for the job.

BASIC WINDOW-DRESSING EQUIPMENT

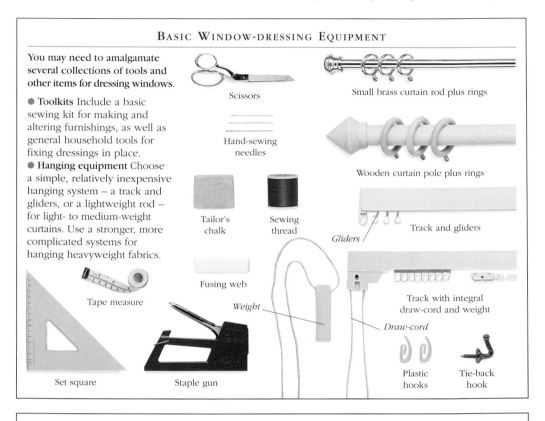

You may need to amalgamate several collections of tools and other items for dressing windows.

● **Toolkits** Include a basic sewing kit for making and altering furnishings, as well as general household tools for fixing dressings in place.
● **Hanging equipment** Choose a simple, relatively inexpensive hanging system – a track and gliders, or a lightweight rod – for light- to medium-weight curtains. Use a stronger, more complicated systems for hanging heavyweight fabrics.

Scissors

Small brass curtain rod plus rings

Hand-sewing needles

Wooden curtain pole plus rings

Tailor's chalk

Sewing thread

Gliders

Track and gliders

Fusing web

Tape measure

Weight

Track with integral draw-cord and weight

Draw-cord

Set square

Staple gun

Plastic hooks

Tie-back hook

CHOOSING FABRICS FOR WINDOW DRESSINGS

Most fabrics can be used for curtains or blinds. Make your choices based on practical as well as aesthetic factors.

● **Colour, pattern, and fibre** Let colours and patterns, or the weave of fabric such as damask, guide your choice, but bear in mind practical factors also.
● **Weight** Choose heavy fabric such as brocade for sumptuous drapes. Sheer silk or fine fabrics such as lace, cotton, or calico will be more light and airy.
● **Function** If using thin curtain fabric, consider lining to block light or interlining for warmth.

Brocade

Cotton

Calico

Damask

Lace

Silk

CHOOSING CURTAINS

Y OU DO NOT HAVE TO BE an expert at sewing to make curtains. Not all curtains have to be lined or hemmed. It is possible to adapt many curtaining techniques to suit your level of ability and still achieve the look you would like.

CONSIDERING OPTIONS

Curtains offer a lot of scope when it comes to covering windows. They come in many different materials, styles, and designs. You can make them, buy them ready-made, or adapt existing ones. Consider your preferences as well as practical requirements before you decide.

PLANNING CURTAINS

● **Lining** You do not have to line curtains, but if you do so it will improve the hang and provide the room with extra warmth. To avoid sewing lining in, attach it to curtain material using fusing web.
● **Avoiding obstacles** Pipes, radiators, and other obstacles or restrictions may prevent curtains from falling nicely. Take these into account when determining the style and the length of your curtains.
● **Selecting hanging systems** Choose a hanging system before you measure up for curtains, since the drop will clearly affect your calculations.

CHOOSING CURTAIN LENGTH

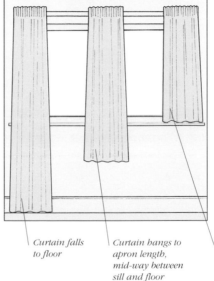

Curtain falls to floor *Curtain hangs to apron length, mid-way between sill and floor* *Curtain hangs just above sill*

Weighing up windows
While you are choosing a style and material for your curtains, consider the ideal length. This will be determined by a number of factors, not least of which are the shape and size of the window itself, the position of a window on a wall, and practical purposes that curtains serve such as keeping a room warm or cool, or blocking light out of it.

CALCULATING FABRIC REQUIREMENTS

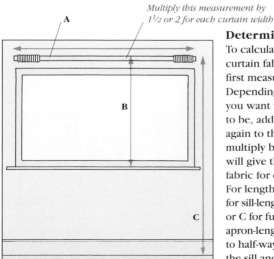

Multiply this measurement by 1½ or 2 for each curtain width

A

B

C

Determining size
To calculate the curtain fabric required, first measure width A. Depending on how full you want the curtains to be, add half as much again to this figure, or multiply by two. This will give the width of fabric for each curtain. For length, measure B for sill-length curtains or C for full-length. For apron-length, measure to half-way between the sill and floor.

MEASURING UP

Measure up as accurately as possible to reduce the risk of making expensive mistakes.

● **Checking figures** The old adage about measuring twice and cutting once is wise advice. Always check your figures because mistakes are easily made when taking a number of measurements.
● **Being precise** Not all floors, windows, and ceilings are absolutely "square", so take at least three width and length measurements.
● **Allowing for pattern repeats** As with wallpaper, centralize large patterns for balance.

CURTAINING CREATIVELY

Window dressings, and curtains particularly, offer a good opportunity to break with tradition and create your own designs and decorative themes. You can, of course, make or buy new curtains, but there are many ways of adapting and revamping existing curtains.

REDUCING COSTS

● **Reviving old curtains** Give old curtains a new lease of life simply by attaching some new braid or trim to their hems.
● **Cutting down curtains** To give a room a fresh new look, make some café curtains by cutting down an old pair of curtains from a different room in your home.
● **Using old for new** To save time and money, use old curtains as a lining around which to fit new fabric. Enclose the old in the new and simply secure around the edges with fusing web.
● **Buying seconds** There is quite a market in second-hand curtains. Consider buying second hand to reduce your expenses significantly. You may, however, have to make size adjustments for the curtains to fit your windows.

IMPROVING HEMS

● **Weighting** Make lightweight curtains hang better by placing coins or purpose-made weights inside hem corners, or gluing decorative beads along the outside edges of the hems.

Roll up fringed trim from one end

Making a tassel

Make a tassel by carefully rolling up some excess trim or braid and securing it with fabric glue. Insert a length of cord and use as a tie-back, or hang several tassels from a curtain rail to dress it up.

MONEY-SAVING TIP

Using a sheet

Use a sheet as a simple, single curtain. Nail the sheet to the top of a window frame using large, exterior roofing nails. Drape the "curtain" to one side of the window over another roofing nail which is used as a tie-back.

USING OTHER MATERIALS

Consider how a curtain will hang when you are planning to use alternative materials, and keep headings simple.

● **Blankets** Use blankets as heavyweight "curtains" in very cold rooms. The insulatory properties of blankets make them ideal.
● **Hessian** Sew hessian sacks into a patchwork to create a rustic but very natural-looking window dressing.
● **Rugs** If you have a window with a poor outlook, use a decorative rug as a window dressing and a distraction. Make use of a rug's looped fringe to hang the rug from a substantial curtain pole.

USING APPLIQUÉ

Attaching shapes

Brighten up a plain material by cutting themed shapes out of a differently coloured fabric. Attach the shapes to the curtain using fabric glue. Use a non-fraying fabric such as felt for the shapes to avoid finishing edges.

DECORATING SHEERS

Tracing outlines

Use sheer curtain fabric like a piece of tracing paper. Draw straight on to the material using a colourfast outliner pen. Leaves are an easy subject to draw around. Fix the outliner ink by ironing the back of the fabric.

HANGING CURTAINS

There are two main methods of hanging curtains: using poles or using tracks. Most types are straightforward to fix in place. You can, however, adapt either of these basic systems in order to add a touch of originality or to suit a particular decorative or colour scheme.

USING POLES

● **Selecting materials** Choose a wooden pole for a fresh, lightweight appearance, or a sturdier-looking metal pole for a more solid, heavy look.

Carefully roll paper around pole

Covering poles

Cover a pole with wallpaper to match the walls. Attach the paper with neat PVA, let it dry, then apply several coats of matt varnish to protect the paper and facilitate curtain pulling.

MEASURING & FIXING

● **Adjusting width** Adjust the length of a curtain pole depending on whether the curtains will be gathered back beyond the edge of the window, or whether they will hang partly in front of the window and therefore require a shorter length of pole.
● **Allowing for finials** Do not forget to allow for finial attachments at each end when calculating a pole's length.
● **Making poles level** You will require only two brackets – one at each end – to fix a curtain pole in position above a narrow window. It will be easy to ensure that the brackets are level using a spirit level. It is more difficult to align three brackets. Fix the central bracket first, and use this to take a level to where the other two need to be positioned.

ALTERNATIVE TO USING POLES

You can choose from a variety of alternative materials as substitutes for curtain poles. Alternatively, use your imagination and substitute a less obvious but still suitable item instead of a pole.

● **Driftwood** Use a slender length of driftwood to make a pole suitable for draping either curtains or swags.
● **Copper pipes** These make ideal curtain poles. You can bend them to fit around corners, so use them in bay and dormer windows.
● **Bamboo canes** Use bamboo canes as an inexpensive means of hanging lightweight, sheer curtain fabrics.
● **Pole supports** Use ornate shelf brackets to support any kind of pole and to provide a decorative finish.

ALTERNATIVES TO USING HEADING TAPE

With a little imagination you can substitute all sorts of items for standard heading tape when hanging curtains. Make holes in fabric with a punch-and-rivet set to facilitate the threading of ties.

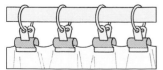

Bulldog clips
Hang bulldog clips from curtain rings. Paint them if you wish.

Bow-tie ribbons
Cut ribbons to the same length to ensure consistent loop size.

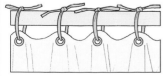

Raffia loops
Tie lengths of raffia or string around a pole for a rustic feel.

Strip of leather
Thread along, with a constant drop from pole to curtain.

USING TRACKS

● **Looking and learning** If you are concerned that you might not be able to assemble and fit a curtain track, have a look at a similar working system, either in your local supplier's showroom or in someone else's home. You will then know what the track should look like once assembled.
● **Painting to match** Consider painting curtain tracks, which are usually supplied white, so that they blend in with wall colours or curtain materials. Eggshell gives the best paint finish on plastic surfaces.
● **Lubricating tracks** In order to maintain a curtain track in good running order, lubricate it occasionally with a few drops of washing-up liquid.

CHOOSING BLINDS

BLINDS ARE THE MAIN ALTERNATIVE TO CURTAINS and can be made from many different fabrics. Try to balance decorative and functional requirements, and assess, for example, to what extent a blind will screen light or provide privacy.

STYLES OF BLIND

Blinds vary in shape and size as much as any other kind of window dressing, and may be left plain or decorated extravagantly depending on your own preferences and practical requirements. These factors affect both the material you choose for your blind and the hanging mechanism you will need.

Roller
Roller blinds are the most functional and require least material.

Austrian
Austrian blinds use more fabric and suit opulent decorative schemes.

Roman
Roman blinds consist of subtle, gently folded layers of material.

Venetian
Venetian or slatted blinds can be plastic, metal, or wooden.

MEASURING UP

Techniques for measuring up for blinds depend upon whether you prefer a flat blind or one that consists of folds of fabric. The surface area will be determined by whether the blind will hang inside or outside a recess as well as by the size of the window itself.

MEASURING FOR BLINDS IN RECESSED WINDOWS

● **Fixing attachments** Decide on the position of a blind, and fit the pole or track before you take the measurements for material. Your calculations will then be more accurate.

● **Overestimating** Err on the side of generosity when calculating amounts of material. It is better to have to trim than start afresh because you do not have enough material.

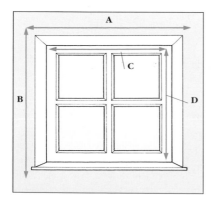

Measuring a recess
For a roller blind outside a recess, measure the width (A), including a 3-cm (1¼-in) overlap on to the walls, and the length (B) to below the sill. Add 5 cm (2 in) for attaching the fabric to a dowel. For a blind inside a recess, allow for brackets in the width measurement (C). Calculate length (D) to above the sill.

MEASURING AUSTRIANS

● **Calculating width** Tape the end of a long length of string to one corner at the top of a window frame. Take the string along the frame to the other corner, forming a number of scallop shapes. Measure the length of string to give you the width of the blind including ruched folds. Add an extra 20 cm (8 in) for side turnings.
● **Measuring length** Add 30 cm (12 in) to the basic height measurement to allow for the depth of the scalloped edge when the blind is down.
● **Counting scallops** Bear in mind that an odd number of scallops creates a more balanced look than an even number.

MAKING AND FITTING BLINDS

Plain roller blinds work by means of a fairly simple mechanism, making them the easiest type of blind both to make and to fit. Most blinds are adapted from this system, although there are alternative types of blind that can be constructed to provide a more individual look.

CHOOSING FABRICS
● **Assessing suitability** For flouncy blinds such as Austrian, choose lightweight materials such as moiré or soft cotton which will ruche well. Heavier fabrics will not gather well.

REVIVING BLINDS
● **Spraying** Paint old Venetian blinds to give them a new lease of life. Wash them in the bath, allow to dry, then spray with an aerosol paint.
● **Stencilling** Transform a plain blind by stencilling it with fabric paints. Make your own stencil, picking out a design from fabrics or other decorations within the room.
● **Dyeing** If a blind remains in good condition but has become discoloured by light, use a cold-water dye in order to transform the look of it completely. Choose a colour to match or tone in with other decorations within the room.

SQUARING CORNERS
● **Making angles** To ensure the smooth running of a roller blind, cut precise, 90-degree angled corners. Use a large set-square and tailor's chalk to draw accurate guidelines.

FIXING MATERIAL

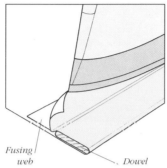

Fusing web   *Dowel*

Avoiding stitching
To make a casing for a wooden dowel at the bottom of a blind without sewing, iron in some fusing web. Secure the material firmly to the roller at the top of the blind using a staple gun.

FINISHING EDGES
● **Preventing fraying** Use a stiffened fabric for roller blinds. This can be cut to an exact size and will not fray. Stabilize lightweight fabric edges with zigzag stitch.

ATTACHING SIMPLY

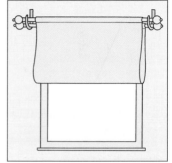

Avoiding a roller system
A mechanical roller system is not essential to "pull" a blind. Attach a dowel at each end of a blind, and a hook in the wall at each end at the top. Rest the lower dowel over the hooks to let light in.

IMPROVISING YOUR OWN SHUTTER BLINDS

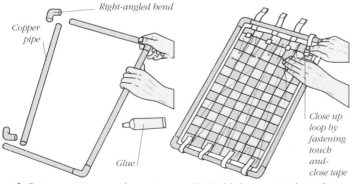

Copper pipe   *Right-angled bend*

Glue

Close up loop by fastening touch and-close tape

1 Cut copper pipes down to the required size using a hacksaw. Use right-angled bends to fit the pipes together to make a frame. Use metal bonding adhesive to make sure that the joints are secure.

2 Hold the material in place in the centre of the frame using a tabbed heading. Secure the tabs with touch-and-close tape. This is ideal since the material can be removed easily and cleaned as required.

3 Use standard pipe brackets as hinges. Attach two brackets on each side of the frame which will hold the shutters secure but also allow enough movement for them to be opened and closed.

ADDING TRIMMINGS

M ANY OF THE TRIMMINGS for window dressings are purely decorative and are used as accessories to a colour scheme or style. Other trimmings, however, are dual-purpose and perform a function within a window-dressing system.

PELMETS

P elmets form a decorative finish to hide the running systems of curtains and create a finished-looking window dressing. They tend to be used for grand curtain treatments, but lighter-weight, less elaborate versions can look effective in a simpler decorative scheme.

USING PELMETS

● **Papering pelmets** Decorate plain wooden pelmets simply by painting or wallpapering them. Use the same paper as that covering the walls, which will make the job easier and less costly than using fabric.

● **Increasing impact** Add a decorative moulding around the top of a pelmet, or use the pelmet as a shelf for displaying ornaments to increase its visual impact.

● **Creating effects** Use a pelmet to alter a window's apparent shape. Position it above the top of the window dressing, for example, to make the window seem taller.

SHAPING PELMETS

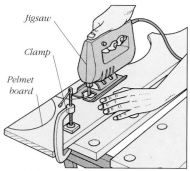

Jigsaw

Clamp

Pelmet board

Using a jigsaw
Add to the decorative appeal of a wooden pelmet by scalloping the lower edge. Mark out the curved design on the pelmet board, clamp the pelmet on to a workbench, and use a jigsaw carefully to cut the shapes.

ATTACHING FABRIC PELMETS

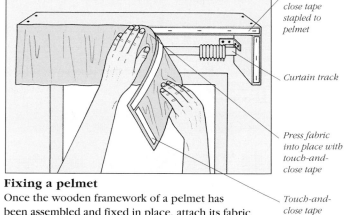

Touch-and-close tape stapled to pelmet

Curtain track

Press fabric into place with touch-and-close tape

Touch-and-close tape fixed to fabric

Fixing a pelmet
Once the wooden framework of a pelmet has been assembled and fixed in place, attach its fabric front. Ideally, make this piece with a flexible buckram frame so that it is easy to fit in place, and can be held there using touch-and-close tape.

VALANCES

A valance serves a similar purpose to a pelmet, but it is constructed from fabric rather than a solid material. Despite being less substantial, a valance can contribute to the decorative impact of a window dressing.

● **Saving money** Make a valance rather than a pelmet if you are working within a tight budget. The fabric needed for a valance will cost much less than a more substantial alternative.

● **Using ceilings** In a room with a low ceiling, you can hang a valance directly from the ceiling without a rail. Attach hooked screw fixings directly to the valance's heading tape.

Hanging a valance alone
A valance is highly decorative and can be hung by itself – without curtains – as a finish in its own right. Fix it in position using a valance rail so that the fabric will hang with a good shape and be seen to the best effect.

SWAGS AND TAILS

Swags and tails can either accompany a pelmet or be used alone as a decorative window dressing. These decorative items take the pelmet and valance idea a stage further. Their function is purely decorative, but they can be used imaginatively to great effect.

MAKING SIMPLE SWAGS

Using door knockers
Creat a simple swag effect by fixing an ornate door knocker above each top corner of a window. Drape material around the window through the rings so that it hangs in a flowing style.

BEING INVENTIVE
● **Using alternative materials**
Since swags are usually simply draped, experiment with different kinds of material. Try long silk scarves, saris, or other lightweight fabrics to create all sorts of voluminous and shapely draped effects.
● **Draping in position** For an informal hanging system, simply drape your material around a pole or other curtain-hanging mechanism. Make a few stitches in appropriate places to maintain the hold.
● **Creating pleats** When attaching swags and tails to a pelmet, use a staple gun. This will allow you to secure the fabric and create neat pleats easily to improve the way the material falls.

BRIGHT IDEA

Using leftovers
Leftover pieces of material need never go to waste. You can use even the smallest slithers of material left over from making trimmings to add a co-ordinating or contrasting frilled edging around a plain cushion.

TIE-BACKS

The traditional function of a tie-back is to hold a window dressing back to one side of a window (or door) in order to allow light in. Tie-backs can, however, also have a decorative role, as an integral part of the window dressing or even as decorations in their own right.

USING TIE-BACKS
● **Using contrasting fabric** In a formal curtain arrangement that includes a pelmet, for example, use a different fabric for the tie-backs and pelmet, to add definition to the curtains.
● **Tying easily** Choose ribbons or cords for the simplest of material tie-backs. Hold them secure by looping them over hooks screwed into the wall.
● **Positioning tie-backs** In the case of tall windows, tie-backs are best positioned about one-third of the way up the wall. Experiment with string before you finalize the position. This will also enable you to judge the length of the tie-back.

USING ALTERNATIVE MATERIALS IN TIE-BACKS

Being creative with leaves
Entwine wired artificial leaves together to create an unusual and attractive tie-back resembling a wreath. Spray the leaves using aerosol paints to co-ordinate them with the colour scheme.

Using a door knob
A door knob makes an ideal tie-back as long as curtain material is not too heavy and does not fall over it. If it does, attach a block of wood to the back of the knob to make it more substantial.

DECORATING GLASS

Window dressings are not the only way of decorating windows; you can decorate the glass itself. The design of stained glass windows ranges from gothic to modern, so you will have a wealth of tradition on which to draw.

BASIC EQUIPMENT AND MATERIALS

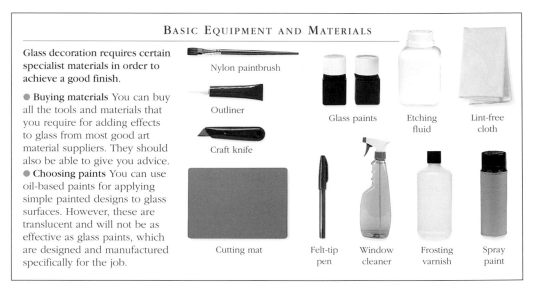

Glass decoration requires certain specialist materials in order to achieve a good finish.

● **Buying materials** You can buy all the tools and materials that you require for adding effects to glass from most good art material suppliers. They should also be able to give you advice.

● **Choosing paints** You can use oil-based paints for applying simple painted designs to glass surfaces. However, these are translucent and will not be as effective as glass paints, which are designed and manufactured specifically for the job.

Nylon paintbrush

Outliner

Craft knife

Glass paints

Etching fluid

Lint-free cloth

Cutting mat

Felt-tip pen

Window cleaner

Frosting varnish

Spray paint

ETCHING WINDOWS

Etched windows are traditionally used in bathrooms, cloakrooms, and entrance halls in order to provide privacy as well as decoration. Etched glass can look effective in any window, but it is particularly useful if the window is very plain or overlooks an undesirable area.

USING FROSTING VARNISH

● **Cleaning windows** Before varnishing, clean a window with household cleaner so that the glass surface is free of grime and other impurities.

● **Applying varnish** Apply frosting varnish using the basic stencilling method (see p. 35). Fix a stencil in position on the window with a light covering of spray-on adhesive, and then apply the varnish to the outlined design.

● **Changing designs** Most frosting varnishes are acrylic, so you can easily modify or completely change a design simply by cleaning away the varnish using an abrasive cleaner and a window scraper.

ETCHING QUICKLY

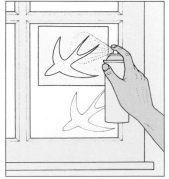

Using spray-on "snow"
With a stencil in place on a window, use spray-on festive snow for an etched effect. Two or three light coats are better than one thick one. Remove excess snow with fine sandpaper.

GREEN TIP

Reusing etching fluid
Proprietary etching fluids can be used on any glass surface. Most can be reused, since once the fluid has dried, the residue can be scraped away, returned to the pot, and used again in the future.

REPRODUCING STAINED-GLASS EFFECTS

Modern decorating materials make it relatively easy to reproduce the effect of stained glass on your windows without having to use coloured glass or lead. You can use proprietary paints on plain glass to achieve a very authentic-looking stained-glass effect.

CREATING DESIGNS

● **Seeking inspiration** Having chosen a window to decorate, you must then select a design. Stained glass is traditionally associated with ornate settings and religious themes, while single motifs or original patterns on plain glass windows are a more modern option.

● **Tracing designs** Fix a design outline to the outside of a window using a low-tac adhesive. Draw the design on thick card so that it is rigid enough to remain in place against the glass surface, making tracing much easier.

● **Finishing off** Once it is dry, clean your stained glass using a soft cloth and mild household window cleaner.

IMITATING STAINED GLASS ON A WINDOW

1 Fix a design to the outside of a window. Apply the appropriate colour to each area on the inside. Do not overload the brush since the paint will run easily. Work from the top down to avoid smudging.

2 Once the colours are dry, add the leaded effect using a tube of silver outliner. Keep a steady movement to avoid unevenness. Remove the design from the outside of the window when you have finished.

REPRODUCING LEADED-LIGHT EFFECTS

Leaded lights share a similar tradition to that of stained glass, although the technique for reproducing them is quite different. A leaded-light effect is ideal for large, plain windows that lack interesting features or for recreating a period look as part of a decorative theme.

CREATING LEADED LIGHTS ON YOUR WINDOWS

1 Draw the leaded-light design on clear sticky-backed plastic, and attach it to the inside of the window. Cut around the "panes" of glass, leaving them stuck to the glass but peeling away the rest.

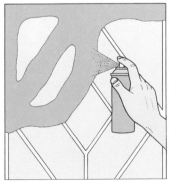

2 With a proprietary metallic aerosol paint, apply three or four thin coats to the entire area. Metallic paint is ideal since it adds texture and depth to the leaded areas as well as providing a realistic colour.

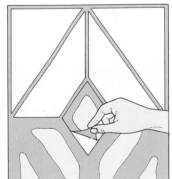

3 When the paint is dry, remove the "panes" of sticky-backed plastic between the "leaded" strips to reveal the glass. Remove any excess drips or runs of paint using a standard window scraper.

FINISHING TOUCHES

THE MAJORITY OF DECORATIVE SCHEMES *are incomplete without a few final flourishes to complement and enhance the finish. Lighting, wall decorations, shelving, and soft furnishings can all be used for this purpose. Many such items have a mainly ornamental function, allowing you to indulge personal taste and add individuality to your decorative scheme.*

CONSIDERING OPTIONS

It is up to you how much you accessorize, but you will need to take certain factors into account when making any decisions. You can usually achieve a desired effect in a number of ways, and which one you should choose may depend on the function of a particular room.

DISPLAYING ITEMS
● **Adding interest** Create an inviting atmosphere in areas of the home used for recreation by hanging wall decorations, and displaying ornaments and other interesting items.

TAKING TIME
● **Building up a scheme** Do not rush to add the finishing touches to a room. Once the main decorating has been completed, you can introduce further additions over time.

USING UNDERSTATEMENT
● **Choosing carefully** In a minimalist decorative scheme, keep the accessories to a minimum also. Finishing touches will be conspicuous, so select them very carefully.

SAFETY

When carrying out any of the tasks outlined in this chapter, be sure to take appropriate safety precautions.

● **Electricity** Do not allow anyone other than a fully trained, qualified electrician to carry out electrical work.
● **Pipes and wires** These are usually visible, but may run behind a wall surface. Check for pipes and wires before hanging pictures and mirrors.
● **Fire hazards** Choose fire-retardant materials, or have their surfaces treated.
● **Harmful substances** Some products contain harmful substances that must not touch the skin or be inhaled. Follow manufacturers' guidelines.

USING LOTS OF ITEMS

Providing variety
A clutter of ornaments and other items can be used to create a comfortable, homely feel. Leave space to move, and do not use too many colours. Here, warm, natural woods balance cool blues.

MINIMIZING EXTRAS

Creating harmony
In a bedroom, keep ornaments and other items to a minimum and harmonize colours for a restful feeling. Here, matching covers and cushions, for example, create a harmonious atmosphere.

LIGHTING

LIGHTING DOES FAR MORE THAN JUST PRODUCE LIGHT. It is one of the most influential tools for creating mood and atmosphere in a room, and there is an extensive range of options to choose from to achieve effects you like.

LIGHTING TYPES

Although styles of lighting vary considerably, there are only a few categories – based largely on function – into which the majority of lighting systems fall. Within these groups, designers have excelled in producing lighting to suit all tastes, and lighting styles and fashions contribute greatly to the overall decorative look of a room.

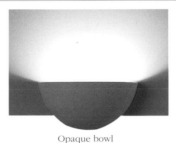
Opaque bowl

Pendant with shade

Tungsten reflector

Desk light with clamp

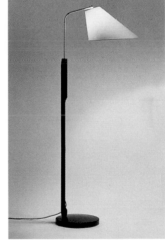
Brass standard lamp with paper shade

Wooden base with paper shade

ENERGY-EFFICIENT TYPES OF LIGHTBULB

Energy-efficient lightbulbs produce an attractive light and last up to five times longer than conventional bulbs.

● **Fluorescent** Substitute these for standard domestic bulbs.
● **Tungsten-halogen** These are low-voltage with purpose-built fittings. Choose them for powerful yet unobtrusive lighting, such as in a kitchen.

Tungsten-halogen bulbs

2-D miniature fluorescent bulb

Bayonet cap fitting

Screw fitting

Fluorescent bulbs

Miniature, low-voltage reflector

Mains-voltage reflector

FIXED LIGHTING

Most rooms have some fixed lighting which is usually operated by switches located close to a door or entrance. In spite of this relatively limited set-up, there are numerous ways in which fixed lighting can be adapted in order to achieve more interesting light effects.

CHOOSING LIGHTS

● **Changing pendant lights** Consider changing a pendant light fitting to sunken or track-mounted spotlights. These can totally change a room's mood.

● **Lighting alcoves** Fixed lighting is ideal for showing off room features and displays. Chasing in new electrical cables might necessitate redecoration, so consider battery-powered lighting, especially for occasional use.

● **Diffusing light** Paint and suspend a metal colander from the base of a lampshade. It will channel the light into many shafts, creating shadows and a varied intensity of light.

MAKING A STRIP-LIGHT DIFFUSER

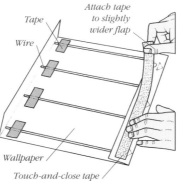

Tape · Wire · Attach tape to slightly wider flap · Wallpaper · Touch-and-close tape

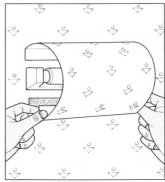

1 Cut some wallpaper to size, and strengthen by taping lengths of wire across it. Fold the long edges of wallpaper to form two flaps, and attach touch-and-close tape to them.

2 Attach lengths of touch-and-close tape above and below the light. Gently bend the wired wallpaper to form a half-cylinder. Position it around the light and fasten the tape.

DIRECTIONAL LIGHTING

Directing light can significantly enhance the decorative scheme in a room, or highlight specific features and thereby create a localized area of special interest. Directional lighting is also useful when you are reading or for work purposes, and therefore serves a dual function.

FOCUSING LIGHT

Creating a specific effect
Use uplighters to draw the eye upwards, increasing the "height" of a room. Ensure that the ceiling is very well decorated, however, since concentrated light will highlight imperfections.

CONSIDERING USAGE

Mixing style and function
Choose bedside lighting that is atmospheric but also allows you to read adequately. An extending base on this wall light enables you to direct light, and fits into a modern decorative scheme.

ADAPTING LIGHTING

● **Using dimmers** Vary the intensity of directional light by using dimmer switches. These can be installed relatively inexpensively and will enable you to increase or decrease the amount of light in a room by a simple turn of the switch.

● **Hiding lights** Blend lights into their surroundings to create a harmonious and relaxed effect. For example, paint opaque bowl wall lights to match the wall colour.

● **Using spotlights** These provide the most adaptable form of directional lighting since you can point them in any direction. Change the emphasis of lighting within a room by occasionally altering the direction of spotlights.

LAMPSHADES

Once you have chosen your light fittings, consider how lampshades will affect the kind of light produced and the co-ordination of lighting with other decorative features. You can buy a shade as part of a lighting system, or make or adapt your own for a personal note.

CONTRASTING SHADES

Using different colours
As in all aspects of decor, the colour of a lamp and its shade will affect the atmosphere and style of a room. Use strongly contrasting colours to make a localized decorative statement.

ENHANCING SHADES

Cut out shape enhances plain lampshade

Introducing shapes
Add interest to plain lamps and shades by adapting their designs. For example, cut simple patterns or shapes into a lampshade, perhaps linking to other designs and motifs within the room.

USING LAMPSHADES

● **Directing light** Line a lampshade with dark paper to channel light through the bottom and top openings and therefore create concentrated, directional shafts of light.
● **Varying colour** Alter the effect of a lampshade by using a coloured lightbulb. This will have a dramatic effect if you are using a pale lampshade, and allow you to experiment with colour and a dark shade.
● **Keeping clean** To ensure that a lampshade looks at its best, always keep it clean. Either vacuum it using the appropriate attachment or wrap sticky tape around your hand (sticky-side out) and brush over the surface of the shade to pick up dust and dirt.

DECORATING SHADES

● **Attaching stickers** Stick shaped, fluorescent stickers on to a plain lampshade. Once they have absorbed light while the lamp is on, they will continue to shine when it has been turned off. This is a particularly good idea in a child's bedroom.
● **Stencilling designs** Co-ordinate lampshades with the rest of the decoration in a room by stencilling the same design on a shade as there is on a border, for example.
● **Using a wallpaper border** Cut down a wallpaper border to make a mini-border, and attach it around the edges of colour-co-ordinating shades.
● **Adding trimmings** Use contrasting or matching braid, tassels, or other appropriate trimmings to enhance the lower edge of a plain shade.

THREADING A SHADE WITH DECORATIVE STRANDS

● **Making holes** A hole punch intended for paper will not cut lampshade material adequately so use a leather punch to make however many holes you need.

● **Choosing threads** Once you have made the holes, change the ribbon or thread occasionally to reflect festive or other special occasions.

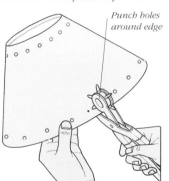

Punch holes around edge

1 Use a pencil to make a series of equidistant marks around the upper and lower edges of a lampshade. Make holes at these marks using a leather punch, holding the shade firmly as you do so.

2 Pass some ribbon through the holes, making a criss-cross pattern over the surface of the lampshade. Create any number of your own designs using the same method and a variety of alternative materials.

SHELVING

SHELVING IS ESSENTIALLY FUNCTIONAL, and its size and degree of sturdiness will depend on load-bearing requirements. But it can also be a design accessory which, within the constraints of practicality, you can decorate as you like.

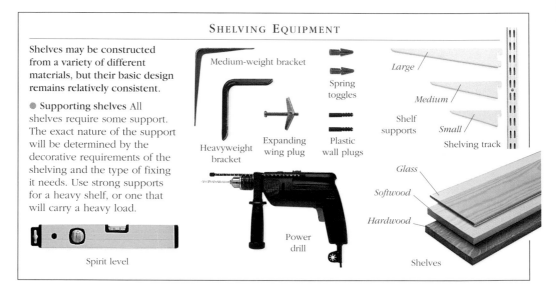

SHELVING EQUIPMENT

Shelves may be constructed from a variety of different materials, but their basic design remains relatively consistent.

● **Supporting shelves** All shelves require some support. The exact nature of the support will be determined by the decorative requirements of the shelving and the type of fixing it needs. Use strong supports for a heavy shelf, or one that will carry a heavy load.

Medium-weight bracket

Spring toggles

Large

Medium

Heavyweight bracket

Expanding wing plug

Plastic wall plugs

Shelf supports

Small

Shelving track

Glass

Softwood

Hardwood

Power drill

Spirit level

Shelves

FIXING SHELVES

Apart from certain types of freestanding unit, a shelf will always need firm wall fixings to hold it in position. Be sure to use a fixing that is appropriate for the type of wall, since particular designs of screw are intended for specific types of construction materials.

Searching for obstructions
Before attaching any shelf fixings into a wall, use a small metal detector to ensure that there are no wires or pipes beneath the surface. Such metal detectors are relatively inexpensive to buy.

INSERTING WALL PLUGS
● **Limiting drilling** When drilling holes, measure the length of the wall plug against the drill bit. Place a piece of sticky tape around the bit at this point so that you can see when you have drilled the correct distance into the wall.
● **Knocking in plugs** If it is necessary, use the handle end of a hammer to knock plugs into a wall. Using the striking face can damage the plugs.
● **Rectifying overdrilling** If a hole is too large or a wall surface crumbles so that the hole widens, fill the hole with proprietary filling adhesive and then insert the plug. Let it dry before inserting the screw.

KEEPING SHELVES LEVEL

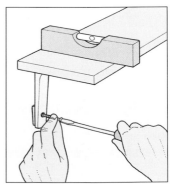

Packing out a bracket
If a shelf slopes forwards due to the unevenness of the wall, pack out its brackets with pieces of cardboard. Place a spirit level on top of the shelf to help you judge how much packing to use.

DECORATING SHELVES

Shelves can be treated like any other item in a room in that they may be decorated in order to blend, complement, or contrast with their surroundings. When deciding how to decorate them, consider to what extent they will be obscured by items placed on them.

COVERING SHELVES

● **Allowing drying time** After painting shelves, let at least 72 hours pass before putting anything on them. This lets the paint dry completely, preventing denting or scraping when you place ornaments.

● **Adding trimmings** Decorate edges of shelves with material trim or a row of upholstery pins for a textured finish.

● **Using plastic** To produce a hardwearing yet decorative surface, cover the tops of shelves with patterned sticky-backed plastic. This is ideal for kitchen shelves which require regular cleaning. Alternatively, apply wallpaper to shelves and finish with several coats of varnish.

ADDING DECORATIVE MOULDINGS

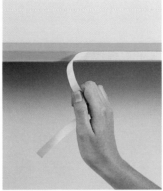

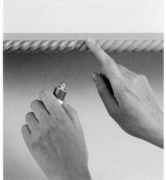

1 Attach double-sided tape along the front edge of the shelf. Cut a piece of moulding to the required length and stick it to the shelf edge. The tape eliminates the need for nails so no filling is required.

2 Apply gilding cream along the moulding's surface. For the best effect, highlight parts of the moulding rather than covering it totally with cream. Vary the extent to which the base colour shows through.

IMPROVISING SHELVES

Adaptation and variation are the keys to the creation of individual decorative schemes. Shelving provides an excellent opportunity to develop your innovative ideas. Its simple construction, requiring limited technical skills, means you can design and build from scratch.

USING ALTERNATIVES

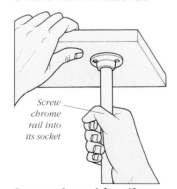

Screw chrome rail into its socket

Supporting with rails

Improvise vertical supports between shelves with chrome towel rails. While not designed for this purpose, they provide adequate support and create a very modern, alternative look.

SERVING PRACTICALITIES

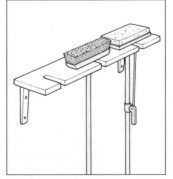

Storing equipment

Many household objects are awkwardly shaped and difficult to store. Adapt a plain shelf by cutting out holes along its front edge from which to hang brooms and mops, for example.

BEING INVENTIVE

● **Creating freestanding shelves** Shelves need not be secured to a wall as long as they are sturdy, not too tall, and do not carry heavy loads. Improvise shelving using large terracotta plant pots as supports for lengths of natural wood.

● **"Solidifying" shelves** Make open shelving look more solid by painting the back wall the same colour as the shelves.

● **Hanging from the ceiling** Create an unusual shelving system for light loads by suspending it from the ceiling instead of using wall brackets. If you use chains with hook-and-eye fixings, secure them firmly in supporting beams.

WALL DECORATIONS

Pictures and other wall decorations make a statement about your taste, while the manner in which they are displayed contributes to a room's decorative atmosphere. The wide choice available allows a huge variety of effects.

BASIC HANGING EQUIPMENT

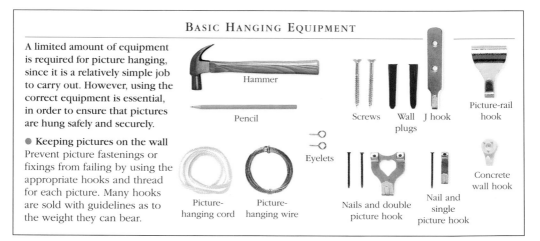

A limited amount of equipment is required for picture hanging, since it is a relatively simple job to carry out. However, using the correct equipment is essential, in order to ensure that pictures are hung safely and securely.

● **Keeping pictures on the wall** Prevent picture fastenings or fixings from failing by using the appropriate hooks and thread for each picture. Many hooks are sold with guidelines as to the weight they can bear.

Hammer

Pencil

Screws

Wall plugs

J hook

Picture-rail hook

Eyelets

Picture-hanging cord

Picture-hanging wire

Nails and double picture hook

Nail and single picture hook

Concrete wall hook

CHOOSING HANGING SYSTEMS

Any wall-hanging system needs to be appropriate for the size of a picture and its weight, which is determined by its mount and frame. Once you have worked this out, you can decide whether the hanging system itself is to be a decorative feature or purely functional.

HANGING INVENTIVELY

● **Using picture rails** Picture rails are ideal for hanging pictures – especially heavy ones – by means of chains, picture wire, or heavyweight cord. For aesthetic effect, consider painting chains so that they match the colour of the walls, or blending in decorative cords with the soft furnishings in the room.

● **Deceiving the eye** Paint a cord between vertically aligned pictures or items such as plates to produce the *trompe l'oeil* effect of them hanging from each other.

● **Avoiding holes** Attach very small, lightweight pictures to a wall using self-adhesive pads rather than a hanging system. This will eliminate the need to knock holes in the wall.

ATTACHING WIRE

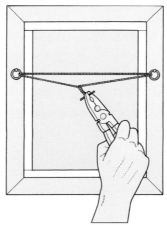

Twisting with pliers
Wire is the most secure means of hanging pictures. Thread wire through an eyelet on each side of a frame. Twist the ends of the wire together using pliers to form a secure and taut fastening.

HANGING ORNATELY

Using ribbon
When displaying plates or other decorative items, make a feature of the hanging system. Wrap wide ribbon around a plate and through a ring. Secure by sewing the ribbon behind the plate.

HANGING WALL DECORATIONS

Positioning wall decorations is important for creating the desired effect in a room. If you do it well, you will not only maintain an overall decorative balance but also ensure that each piece is fully appreciated, fulfilling its role as a finishing touch and a feature in its own right.

ENHANCING PICTURES

● **Lighting** Increase the impact of the pictures within a room by illuminating them with picture lights. Alternatively, use directional spotlights to serve the same purpose.

● **Moving pictures around** Give a room a fresh look by swapping the positions of existing pictures or introducing one or two different ones.

● **Choosing frames** The frame plays an important role in showing off a picture. If you feel you have made a wrong choice of frame, you can modify it quite easily by painting the moulding.

● **Cleaning frames** Frames collect dust and dirt like any other surface. Use an old shaving brush to remove dust and debris from even the most intricate moulding, thereby maintaining the frame in the best possible condition.

DETERMINING POSITION

● **Choosing height** Position pictures for viewing from the eye level of an average-height person. Having to look up or down distorts perspective.

INSERTING HOOKS

Taping over the spot
Apply a piece of masking tape to a wall where a picture hook is to be placed. This will prevent the hook from slipping and reduce the chance of plaster crumbling and the hook being dislodged.

MARKING POSITION

● **Using a finger** Rub chalk on one finger. Position a picture on the wall, then mark the point at which it will hang with the chalked finger.

TRADITIONAL TIP

Sanding a hammer
The striking face of a hammer needs cleaning occasionally to prevent it from slipping off nailheads. Sand the face with fine-grade sandpaper until it is shiny and clean.

USING POSTERS

Although posters are an inexpensive option, they can be used in such a way as to have great decorative impact.

● **Ironing** Use a cool iron to smooth a poster flat before hanging it. Nothing looks worse than a poster that is curling at the edges.

● **Fixing** Attach a poster to a wall using wallpaper adhesive. For the greatest visual impact, place several posters together on one wall, and then apply a coat of varnish over the whole surface for a dead flat finish.

● **Aging** Age posters or prints by rubbing a damp tea bag over the surface of the paper.

HANGING MIRRORS EFFECTIVELY

Mirrors require similar fixings to pictures, except those that sit flush against a wall. Use special corner fixings, mirror pads, or mirror screws in such instances. Take time to consider a mirror's position, as it can dramatically affect the appearance of a room.

● **Hanging large mirrors** Most large mirrors have fixing brackets as an integral part of the frame. Drill rather than nail fixings, and ensure that the size of screws used will be sufficient to take the weight of the mirror.

● **Tightening screws** Take care not to overtighten mirror screws and thus crack the mirror. Insert a thin piece of card behind each screw as a tightening gauge.

Increasing space
Dramatically increase the impression of space in a room by carefully positioning a mirror – especially a large one. Centre it on a wall or in an alcove to distribute its effect evenly over as much of the room as possible.

SOFT FURNISHINGS

Soft furnishings are an integral part of a decorative scheme, contributing to colour co-ordination and style. Complicated upholstering or covering is best left to experts, but in some areas limited skills can achieve effective results.

BASIC EQUIPMENT

A collection of tools necessary for working on soft furnishings is inexpensive to put together. Even the cost of a stapler has come down in price, and there is a good range of high-quality pieces from which to choose.

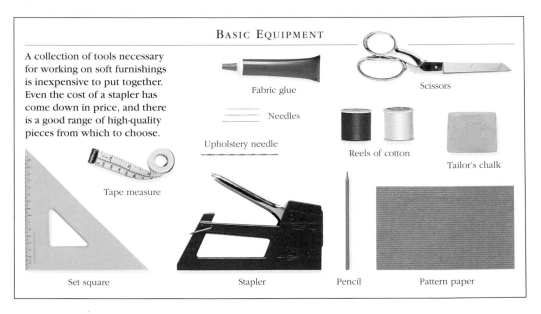

Fabric glue

Scissors

Needles

Upholstery needle

Reels of cotton

Tailor's chalk

Tape measure

Set square

Stapler

Pencil

Pattern paper

CHOOSING FABRICS

Whereas assembling a toolkit is relatively inexpensive, fabrics can send your costs soaring. However, it is up to you to choose how extravagant to be, although in some cases fabric selection will be dictated by the type of finish you require and the look you aim for.

CONSIDERING FABRICS

● **Checking safety** Make sure that material is fire retardant. If it is not, you may need to buy a proprietary spray and treat the material yourself.

● **Choosing colours** It can be difficult to choose fabric when you are not in the room in which it will be used. Paint some of the wall colour on a piece of paper and take it to the shop with you, or take fabric swatches home to view them in the appropriate light conditions and surroundings.

● **Assessing costs** Buy the most expensive fabric that you can afford, since better-quality material is more hardwearing.

COMMON TYPES OF FURNISHING FABRIC

Medium to heavyweight fabrics are the most suitable for making furnishings. They are hardwearing, but you may find that their bulk makes them more difficult to work with than lighter fabrics.

Velvet

Heavyweight cotton

Chenille

Wool mix

USING CUSHIONS AND COVERS

Changing upholstery covers, introducing new cushions, and tying in soft furnishings with the rest of a room's decor can add the perfect finish to a room. How lavish these additions are depends on your preference and sewing ability. Simple ideas can often be very effective.

MAKING CUSHIONS

● **Buying second hand** Buy second-hand curtains and use them to make cushion covers. This is an ideal way of saving money when making more luxurious cushion covers, since plush second-hand material will cost a fraction of the price of the equivalent new fabric.

● **Scenting cushions** Add one or two sprigs of lavender to the stuffing of a cushion to keep it smelling fresh.

● **Cushioning floors** Join two rag rugs together to make a large floor cushion that will be both decorative and practical. Use two different rug designs for a more interesting effect.

● **Making bean bags** Always make an inner lining for a bean bag so that the filling is enclosed in a separate bag, allowing for its easy removal when you want to wash the cover. As an inexpensive alternative filling, use loose-fill loft insulation material.

MEASURING A CHAIR FOR LOOSE COVERS

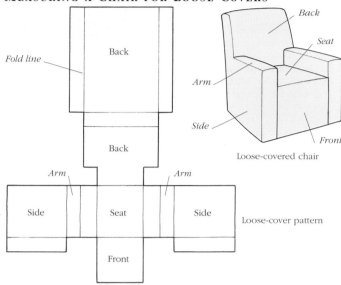

Loose-covered chair

Loose-cover pattern

Making a loose-cover paper pattern

The covering on a chair can be divided up into a number of different sections, depending on the specific design of a chair. Measure the size of each section, and add them all together to give the total area of the chair cover so that you can calculate material quantites. Make a lifesize version of the cover layout from pattern paper, and use it for cutting out the fabric. Remember to make allowances for seams and hems.

CREATING HEADRESTS

Adapting a cushion

Make a metal bedhead more comfortable by attaching a customized cushion to the frame. Sew tabs to the cushion, and use touch-and-close tape or press studs to attach them.

IMPROVING CHAIRS

● **Creating comfort** You may want to make your kitchen chairs more comfortable, especially if the kitchen is the main dining area. Make simple cushions that will provide padding for hard seats.

● **Reviving chairs** Revive an old chair by covering it with a new throw. Alternatively, use a sheet or lightweight rug.

● **Covering arms** Chair arms receive more wear than other parts. Help to keep them in good condition longer by making covers from the same or different material. You can also add a pocket to house a television remote control.

FINISHINGS

Finishing off the material accessories to a decorative scheme is very much a case of knowing how much or how little to use, which is a matter of personal taste. Whether you choose to keep things simple or aim for an extravagant finish, trimmings should enhance a furnishing.

IDEAS FOR TRIMMINGS

There are numerous items – conventional or less so – that can be attached to the soft furnishings in a newly decorated room to add a final finishing touch of creativity.

- Braids.
- Piping and bindings.
- Ribbons.
- Raffia.
- Cord.
- Lace.
- Leather.
- Material offcuts.
- Tassels.
- Fringes.
- Beads.
- Sequins.
- Buttons.
- Bows.
- Chains.
- Clasps and buckles.

FINISHING CUSHIONS

- **Stencilling** You need not confine stencils to walls and woodwork – apply them to cushions or the seats of chairs. This is a good way of tying in painted wall decorations with soft furnishings. It is also a particularly appropriate technique for imitating tapestry on a chair cover. Make sure that you use fabric paints rather than standard acrylics.
- **Edging cushions** Attach trimmings such as braid or piping (using fabric glue) along the edges of cushions, using a variety of colours and shapes to different effect. Add dark-coloured piping to define and highlight the edges of a cushion, or – to soften them – shape the edges into scallops or attach a looped fringe.

BRIGHT IDEA

Hiding stapled edges
Staples can be unsightly and you should disguise them. Attach a length of trim or braid over a line of staples using fabric glue. Press the braid firmly into place so that it maintains its position while the glue dries.

COVERING BEDHEADS

Covering a bedhead is an ideal way to finish off bedroom trimmings. It makes a hard bedhead more comfortable to lean against and can co-ordinate the bed with other decorations in the room. A fabric-covered bedhead may be used to link a bedspread with other furnishings and window dressings.

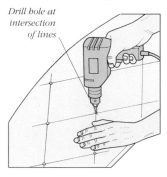

Drill hole at intersection of lines

1 Cut a sheet of MDF to size (wear a dust mask and ensure good ventilation). Draw criss-crossing pencil lines about 15 cm (6 in) apart on one side of the MDF. Drill small holes through where they intersect.

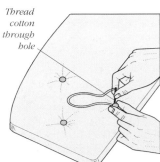

Thread cotton through hole

2 Cut wadding and fabric to size and fit over the MDF, folding enough fabric around the back to staple securely. Attach a length of cotton to a button. Locate the holes and thread the cotton through with a needle.

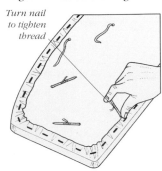

Turn nail to tighten thread

3 Secure the thread around a nail on the back of the MDF. Rotate the nail to adjust the button over the hole at the right tension. Repeat at each drill hole until you have the number of buttons you want.

FINAL DETAILS

T HE PLACING OF OBJECTS in a newly decorated room offers a great opportunity for experimentation. Arranging and displaying ornaments with individual flair will complete the decorative scheme that you planned in the beginning.

═══ ORNAMENTS ═══

O rnaments of all kinds play an important part in our lives, either because they remind us of a special occasion, or they are part of a collection of similar items, or simply because we like them. Whatever the reason, ornaments can have a powerful decorative impact.

CHANGING CONTAINERS

Place soaps in glass jar

Decanting toiletries
Pour shampoo or bubble bath into glass containers, and arrange soaps in a matching jar to turn them into colourful decorative items. Select colours that fit in with the room's colour scheme.

PLACING ORNAMENTS

● **Protecting surfaces** Attach pieces of sticky-backed felt that have been cut to size to the bases of your ornaments – especially heavy ones. This will protect the surface on which they are standing from being scratched as they are moved during cleaning.
● **Arranging items** Ornaments are intended to be seen and should therefore be displayed to maximum effect. Place taller items at the back of a surface so that all items can be seen.
● **Grouping collections** Space objects that form part of a collection carefully in order to show off each individual item as well as the whole group.

SECURING SMALL ITEMS

Attach small piece of tape to base

Using double-sided tape
Lightweight or small ornaments are easily knocked over. Fix them in position by attaching double-sided tape to their bases. Always ensure that the surface on which they stand will not be marked.

BEING PRACTICAL

Adding a finger plate
Screw an ornamental finger plate on to a door for a decorative edge that will protect the door from dirty hands. Finger plates are available in metal, plastic, or decorated ceramic finishes.

DISPLAYING NATURAL MATERIALS

The possibilities are endless for using natural items purely for show or for practical purposes.

● **Seashells** Glue sea shells around the rim of a plant pot for a maritime theme. Paint the pot to suit a colour scheme.
● **Dried flowers** Display dried flowers as they are, or highlight them with gold spray-paint.
● **Pressed flowers** Preserve a bouquet of flowers by pressing it. Use the flowers to create *découpage* effects on ceramics or on pieces of furniture.
● **Feathers** Use feathers in collage displays beneath glass table tops or in simple frames.

Making a soap dish
Cover the base of a ceramic or glass bowl with an assortment of coloured pebbles to make an attractive display, and place a bar of soap on top. Any water will drain through the pebbles to collect at the bottom of the bowl.

TABLEWARE

Table accessories, whether they form part of a permanent display or they are used only occasionally, can contribute effectively to a room's decorative scheme. They also give you the opportunity to use your imagination and bring a touch of originality to your home.

CHANGING USAGE

Press plant gently into cup

Using items as ornaments
Put cups or mugs to novel use by converting them into miniature herb gardens. Extend the idea to other containers for displaying plants. Co-ordinate them to fit in with the decorative scheme.

DECORATING CERAMIC KITCHEN JUGS

Masking tape

1 Create bands around a ceramic jug using masking tape. Remove excess from the sponge before applying acrylic ceramic paint over the whole jug. This will avoid a gummy finish and give depth of colour.

2 Once the paint has dried, remove the tape. This technique can be used to create a variety of designs. To make the jug dishwasher proof, bake in an oven for 40 minutes at 150°C (300°F).

DECORATIVE CONTAINERS

Storage systems often let a decorative scheme down. Even general storage items can be made more attractive by means of a simple decorative overhaul. Boxes and other containers may be hidden away from view, but they too can be transformed into something attractive.

ADAPTING BOXES

● **Painting shoe boxes** Paint shoe boxes to create storage boxes for photographs, letters, or other paperwork. Use vinyl emulsion for a wipeable, hardwearing finish. Choose a different colour for each category of item so that you can identify the contents by the exterior colour of the box.
● **Decorating boxes** Use trimmings to decorate storage boxes. Upholstery studs will give a sturdy look, while glass beads or buttons are colourful.
● **Using packaging** Remove the cardboard divider from a packing box, cut it to size, paint it with emulsion, and insert it in a drawer to create compartments for storing socks or other small items of clothing.

TIDYING BATHROOMS

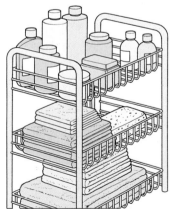

Using a vegetable rack
Most bathrooms are littered with all sorts of bottles and containers. Neaten the room up using a metal vegetable rack which will save space and make it easier to find a particular item.

USING CONTAINERS

● **Storing toys** Hang a simple hammock of a suitable size in a child's bedroom and use it as a quick and easy solution to the problem of storing toys.
● **Doubling up** Create a double-sided storage shelf by attaching jar lids – using either a strong adhesive or screws – to the underside of a shelf. When you have filled them with small items, screw the containers on to their lids so that they hang below the shelf.
● **Using hanging baskets** Turn a hanging basket into a novel type of storage unit rather than using it simply as a plant holder. Hang the basket in a kitchen and use it for storing vegetables, small boxes, or jars of dried herbs and spices.

ROOM DETAILS

Some finishing touches are particularly suited to certain rooms in the home. They tend to add yet another dimension to a completed decorative scheme, but they can also be used to draw together various aspects of a style or simply update and renew an existing look.

CURTAINING OFF CORNERS OF ROOMS

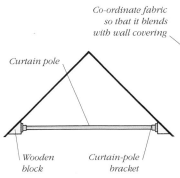

Co-ordinate fabric so that it blends with wall covering

Curtain pole

Wooden block

Curtain-pole bracket

1 Cut a small block of wood diagonally into two pieces. Screw one to each wall just above head height, and about 1 m (3¼ ft) from the corner. Secure a curtain-pole fitting to each block and attach a pole.

2 Paint the blocks to match the wall colour. Hang a curtain from the pole, using a fabric that blends in with the wall decoration. Fit several coat hooks on a rail inside this corner "cupboard" if required.

RENOVATING UNITS

● **Renewing a bath surface** Rather than re-enamelling a bath or replacing it altogether, paint it with a proprietary coating for a new look. Follow manufacturers' guidelines on the preparation of surfaces to ensure the best possible finish.

● **Finishing kitchen cupboards** The look of a kitchen can be transformed by changing or painting drawer and cupboard handles. Go one stage further by renewing the kitchen unit fronts, saving money by retaining the original carcasses if they are in good condition.

● **Revitalizing equipment** Give old, white refrigerators and freezers new life by coating them with coloured proprietary paints. Check manufacturers' instructions to ensure that the surface is suitable. You can also apply paint effects.

USING FABRICS CLEVERLY

Clever use of fabrics will give visual cohesion as well as maximizing space and money.

● **Saving money** Buy a new bedspread or throw to match a colour scheme, rather than replacing all the bed linen.

● **Making a canopy** Attach a curtain pole to the ceiling above a bedhead and another one to the ceiling above the foot of the bed. Drape material between the poles to create a canopy.

● **Screening** Cover a screen with material to match other fabrics in a room, and use it as a movable partition to conceal unattractive features or create a secluded corner.

REINFORCING THEMES WITH ACCESSORIES

Grouping bathroom items with ornaments

Position bathroom accessories simply but effectively to emphasize a theme – in this case a maritime theme and an assortment of blues. The starfish shapes and fish motifs contribute to the theme, while the ceramic fish also provide splashes of contrasting colour.

USEFUL DECORATING TERMS

T HIS GLOSSARY EXPLAINS THE MEANING of common decorating terms that are used but not fully explained in the text of this book. The list includes equipment, materials, decorating methods and techniques, and other useful terms.

● **Acrylic** A term describing decorating materials, such as paint, that are water based.

● **Address** To place a length of pasted wallpaper on a wall ready for manoeuvring into a precise position and attaching.

● **Aging** In decorating, the application of one of a number of techniques to create the impression of wear and tear on a wooden, painted, or plaster surface over a period of time.

● **Antiquing** The application of one of a number of techniques to create the impression of the changes to a wooden, painted, or metal surface over time.

● **Architrave** The moulded edging of a door, window, archway, or wall panel that forms the boundary between that feature and a wall.

● **Austrian blind** A highly decorative window dressing with a scalloped lower edge. The blind is drawn up so as to maintain this shaped edge, and to create the effect of folds of tumbling material.

● **Bagging** A paint-effect technique whereby a crumpled plastic bag is dabbed on a glaze or emulsion to create a pattern.

● **Batten** A length of wood that is square in section and of narrow dimensions, used for a variety of decorative purposes.

● **Bay window** A window that forms a recess in a room, often with three sections looking out in different directions.

● **Bead** To spread paint using a small paintbrush into corner junctions, such as where walls meet ceilings, to create a precise edge between the two.

● **Beading** A thin, wooden, decorative moulding used as an ornamental edging.

● **Bleed** The seepage of unwanted substances, such as resin from wood, through the surface of a painted finish.

● **Blocking** A technique of applying a design to a wall, floor, or other area using a cut-out, shaped object whose surface is dipped in paint and then applied to that area.

● **Bolster chisel** A heavyweight, broad-bladed chisel mainly intended for masonry work, but useful for fitting hessian-backed carpet over gripper rods.

● **Brick bond** A design taken from brick-laying and applied to the laying of tiles, whereby rows of tiles are arranged so that no vertical joins align with those of the previous row.

● **Brocade** A luxurious, heavyweight, silk fabric with a raised design woven into it.

● **Café curtain** A curtain that covers only the lower half of a window, and hangs from a wire or slim curtain pole suspended across the centre of the frame.

● **Calico** A coarsely woven, often unbleached, cotton fabric.

● **Casement window** A window that has vertically hinged sections, and sometimes also includes horizontally hinged and/or fixed sections.

● **Chalk line** A length of string, coated in chalk dust, used to produce accurately positioned, straight guidelines for many decorating tasks. The chalk line may alternatively be housed in a special vessel that contains a chalk reservoir.

● **Chase in** To cut a groove in a wall to take a cable or pipe.

● **Chenille** A thick, velvet-like fabric used for furnishings.

● **Chipboard** A manufactured building board made from compressed wooden particles, used mainly for subfloors.

● **Coir** A coconut-husk fibre used for natural-fibre flooring.

● **Colourwashing** A traditional paint technique whereby paint is diluted and used to create a semi-transparent rather than an opaque finish.

● **Combing** A paint-effect technique whereby a decorator's comb is dragged across a glaze to produce a series of lines.

● **Counter sink** To insert a screw into a wooden surface so that its head does not protrude above that surface. This is achieved by means of a specially designed drill bit.

● **Coving** A decorative plaster or polystyrene moulding used at a wall–ceiling junction.

● **Crackle glaze** A particular type of glaze used to achieve a *craquelure* effect.

● *Craquelure* A French term describing a paint effect used to age a surface with the appearance of a network of fine cracks, and created by the application of varnish to a painted surface.

● **Cut in** To paint the edge of a wall or ceiling to complete the coverage of the surface.

● **Dado rail** A moulding attached along a wall, roughly at waist height, to separate upper and lower areas.

● **Damask** A silk or linen fabric with a design woven into it.

- **Deal** A softwood that is very light in colour and used for most interior joinery.
- *Découpage* A French term describing a technique used to decorate a surface by attaching cut-out paper images to give the impression of painted items.
- **Distressing** One of a number of techniques of deliberately eroding a wooden or painted surface so that it appears worn.
- **Doorstop** A wooden strip that runs around the inside of a door frame, standing proud of it, to provide a barrier against which the door closes.
- **Dowel** A short length of wood, round in section, used for a variety of purposes in decorating and soft furnishings.
- **Dragging** A paint-effect technique whereby a flogger is dragged across a glaze to create a series of very fine lines.
- **Dutch metal** A less expensive alternative to gold leaf, used for gilding purposes.
- **Egg tempera** A traditional egg-yolk-based mixture used as a protective coating for paintwork and paint effects, or mixed with colour to produce a finish in its own right.
- **Eggshell** An oil- or water-based, mid-sheen paint suitable for walls and ceilings.
- **Emulsion** A water-based paint applied mainly to large surfaces such as walls and ceilings.
- *Faux* A French term used when creating paint effects to describe a surface that is very realistically painted to imitate another material, for example wood, ceramic tiles, or marble.
- **Ferrule** The metal strip around the central area of a paintbrush which houses the base of the bristles.
- **Festoon blind** A window dressing similar to an Austrian blind but with gathered scallops throughout the blind's length.
- **Fitch** A small-headed, long-handled brush that is used for

infilling paint details or reaching into inaccessible areas.
- **Flat** A broad surface of a window rail or frame.
- *Fleur-de-lys* A French term describing a traditional motif resembling a lily or iris flower.
- **Flexible filler** A filling compound that is able to absorb minor movements in wood or plaster surfaces and is therefore able to maintain a continuous, smooth, and unbroken paint finish.
- **Flogger** A long-haired paintbrush used to create a dragged paint effect.
- **Flush** A term describing two adjacent surfaces that join without any unevenness, or where a surface is repaired to create a totally level finish.
- **Frame head** The broadest area running around the inside of a wooden door frame which acts as a base for the doorstop.
- **French windows** A casement window or pair of windows that extend to floor level and commonly open outwards on to a garden or other outside area.
- **Fusing web** A mesh-like tape that is used to join two fabric surfaces together but avoids the need for stitching. The fusing process is activated by the heat from an iron.
- **Gilding** A technique of producing a gold surface by the application of either gold leaf or gold paint.
- **Gingham** A fabric with a checked pattern usually created by the weaving of different-coloured yarns.
- **Glaze** An oil- or water-based medium (made by adding a tint to transparent glaze), used for creating paint effects and broken colour finishes.
- **Gloss** A hardwearing, high-sheen paint, mainly used as a top coat on woodwork.
- **Gold leaf** A very thin sheet of rolled or hammered gold that is used for gilding.

- **Graining** A paint-effect technique for creating a realistic natural-wood effect.
- **Grout** A fine plaster or mortar for filling in between tiles to create a flush surface.
- **Hacksaw** A fine-toothed saw used for cutting through metal.
- **Hardboard** A thin manufactured building board made from compressed wooden particles and used mainly for covering subfloors.
- **Hardwood** A wood of higher quality than softwood, used for interior joinery. Good for natural-wood finishes.
- **Hessian** A coarse, plain fabric made from jute fibre.
- **Hue** A variety or degree of a colour. Different hues of a particular colour are often used in the same decorative scheme.
- **Inlay** To insert a contrasting section within a flat surface by filling a hole with a different-coloured material or alternative material, such as wood or tiles, for decorative purposes.
- **Inset tile** A tile of a different design or colour from the surrounding body of tiles.
- **Interlining** An additional layer of muslin or other lightweight material placed next to a fabric to increase insulatory or fire-retardant properties and, in the case of curtains, provide extra bulk to improve the hang.
- **Joist** A large wooden supporting beam used to make a framework on which a floor is constructed.
- **Jute** A plant whose fibre is used for natural-fibre flooring.
- **Knee kicker** A gripping and stretching device that can be used to fit most carpets.
- **Lay off** To brush an unloaded paintbrush across a wet painted surface to disperse the brushmarks in order to create as smooth a finish as possible. Laying off can also be done with a paint roller.

● **Liming** A technique for staining wood a whitish colour using liming wax.

● **Linoleum** A floor covering made from a mixture including linseed oil and resins, mounted on a hessian backing.

● **Load-bearing** Describing the capacity of a structure or item to carry weight.

● **Low-tac** A term usually describing a variety of masking tape that creates just enough adhesion to stick to a surface without damaging that surface when it is removed.

● **Lump hammer** A large hammer with a heavy head, commonly used for masonry.

● **Matt** A term describing a dull finish, commonly associated with emulsion and some natural-wood finishes.

● **Make good** To prepare a surface so that it is ready for decorating.

● **Marbling** A paint-effect technique produced in one of a number of ways to create the impression of a marble surface.

● **Mask** To cover an area – with paper, cardboard, or masking tape – to prevent it from being covered by paint or other decorating material.

● **Medium-density fibreboard (MDF)** A manufactured building board of varying thickness composed of compressed wooden fibres and used for a variety of interior joinery and building tasks.

● **Mitre** To join two pieces of material – for example, tiles or skirting board – at a corner by cutting each at 45 degrees so that they meet neatly.

● **Mural** A large painting or painted decoration on a wall.

● **Muslin** A finely woven cotton fabric.

● **Nail punch** A small metal rod which, when placed vertically over a nail, can be hammered to knock in the nail head below surface level.

● **Natural-fibre flooring** A floor covering made from plant fibre, such as jute, seagrass, coir, or sisal.

● **Nibbler** A hand tool, resembling pliers with sharp teeth, that is used to cut small portions off the edges of ceramic tiles in order to cut them to size or shape them.

● **Nog** A small block of wood that is attached to joists to lend extra support for floorboards.

● **Notched spreader** A tiling tool with a castellated edge used to spread adhesive over a wall prior to attaching tiles.

● **Overspray** A fine spray or splatters of paint that have unintentionally splashed over the wrong surface.

● **Paint effect** The use of paint and other materials to create a pattern, texture, or illusion. A glaze is often the most suitable material, but emulsion can be used as an alternative.

● **Paint system** A method of paint application, using a specific type of paint, required to achieve a particular finish.

● **Parquet flooring** A flooring traditionally made up of small wooden blocks, commonly arranged in a herring-bone or other geometrical pattern. Modern alternatives consist of wooden panels that reproduce the same effect.

● **Pattern repeat** The measurement from where a pattern begins to where it finishes on wallpaper or fabric.

● **Pelmet** A wooden or fabric-covered edging that conceals the hanging system of a window dressing.

● **Picture rail** A moulding that runs along a wall a short distance from the ceiling, over which are hooked devices from which to hang framed wall decorations.

● **Picture window** A window comprising a single, large pane or sheet of glass.

● **Plyboard** A manufactured building board constructed from a number of layers of wood veneer stuck together in such a way that the grain of one layer runs at right angles to that of the previous layer. Also known as ply or plywood.

● **Polyvinyl adhesive (PVA)** A multipurpose adhesive which, when concentrated, acts as a strong glue, but when diluted acts as a stabilizing solution for applying to powdery surfaces.

● **Primary colour** One of three colours – red, blue, and yellow. They are mixed in a variety of ratios to make other colours.

● **Primer** A paint used to seal and stabilize a surface before further coats are applied.

● **Punch-and-rivet set** A hole-making gadget, used on paper or fabric, which leaves a small hole with a rivet finishing.

● **Rag rolling** A paint-effect technique that is similar to ragging except that the rag is made into a sausage-like length and rolled down a glaze or emulsion to produce a directional pattern.

● **Ragging** A paint-effect technique whereby a crumpled rag is used to create a pattern on emulsion or a glaze, or the rag is dipped in emulsion or a glaze, then applied to a surface.

● **Rail** A horizontal or vertical strut that makes up a panelled door or window frame.

● **Rebate** An area of a window rail bordering a pane of glass.

● **Repeat size** The actual dimension of a pattern repeat.

● **Rocker** A paint-effect tool used to create the impression of wood grain.

● **Roman blind** A flat window dressing with a number of horizontal struts that gather the material into a folded concertina as the blind is raised.

● **Rub back** To remove the top coat of a surface to expose what is underneath.

- **Sash window** A window made up of two main parts that slide past each other vertically on sash cords.
- **Sand back** To use sandpaper to level and smooth a surface.
- **Scale down/up** To transfer the outline of a pattern or image from a source on to a flat surface where it will be reproduced by adjusting its size accordingly.
- **Screed** A levelled, concrete surface on which a floor covering is applied.
- **Seagrass** A hardwearing fibre used for natural-fibre flooring.
- **Second fixings** The final attachment of cosmetic and functional fixtures and fittings at the end of a building or decorating project.
- **Secondary colour** A colour made by mixing equal amounts of two primary colours.
- **Self-levelling compound** A compound poured over an uneven floor to produce a level surface.
- **Shade** In everyday usage, a variety or degree of a colour; in scientific terminology, a colour mixed with black.
- **Sheen** The degree to which a particular finish shines.
- **Sheet flooring** A term used to describe a variety of utility flooring that is laid in large continuous sheets, such as linoleum, vinyl, or rubber.
- **Sisal** An agave fibre used for natural-fibre flooring.
- **Size** To prepare a plaster surface with size (diluted wallpaper paste or a PVA solution) to stabilize the surface and ease the manoeuvring of wallpaper once it is on the wall.
- **Soaking time** The period for which wallpaper is left after pasting before hanging, to allow paste to soak in and prevent the formation of bubbles.
- **Softwood** A natural wood that is pale in colour and used for interior joinery.

- **Solvent** The chemical base of certain decorating materials. The term also refers specifically to oil-based paints.
- **Sponging** A paint-effect technique whereby a natural sponge is used to create an impression in a glaze or emulsion, or is used to apply a glaze or emulsion to a wall.
- **Stamping** A technique of applying a design to a wall, floor, or other area using a hand-held block, whose surface bears a design and is dipped in paint and then applied.
- **Stencilling** A decorative technique whereby paint is applied in the cut-out areas of a cardboard or acetate template to create a design on a surface.
- **Stippling** A paint-effect technique whereby the extreme tips of bristles are dipped into a wet glaze to create a velvety texture.
- **Stripper** A solution used to remove old layers of paint from a surface.
- **Subfloor** The surface beneath a flooring, usually of concrete or floorboards, and sometimes covered with hardboard.
- **Swags and tails** Fabric curtain accessories added to a basic window dressing.
- **Template** A design made of paper, cardboard, or acetate that acts as a guide in cutting out a shape from fabric or other materials, or in painting a design on a surface.
- **Tenon saw** A fine-toothed saw that is short in length and is used for joinery purposes.
- **Tertiary colour** A colour made by mixing a primary colour with a secondary one.
- **Tie-back** A material or other device that holds a curtain to one side of a window frame.
- **Tile gauge** A length of wood, calibrated with tile-width measurements and used to mark off the positions that tiles will occupy on a wall.

- **Tint** To adjust the colour of a paint or glaze. Alternatively, in everyday usage, a variety or degree of a colour; in scientific terminology, a colour mixed with white.
- **Tone** A variety or degree of a colour, particularly in terms of its depth or brilliance.
- **Tongue and groove** A system of interlocking wooden planks that are joined to produce a panelled surface.
- *Trompe l'oeil* A French term meaning "trick of the eye" and, in decorating, describing a painted image that gives the impression of a real object.
- **Valance** A decorative fabric edging that conceals the hanging system of a window dressing rather like a pelmet.
- **Varnish** A resinous solution that seals and protects surfaces.
- **Venetian blind** A window dressing consisting of a number of slats of wood, plastic, or other material, the angle of which can be adjusted to control the amount of light passing through.
- **Verdigris** A greenish coating on copper, bronze, or brass that forms naturally with age as a result of corrosion. Its appearance is copied as a decorative effect on metal or wooden surfaces.
- **Vinyl** A soft flooring – in sheets or tiles – that is flexible and cushioned. Alternatively, a type of emulsion.
- **Wood-block flooring** A type of wooden sheet flooring consisting of small blocks.
- **Wood panelling** A wooden wall covering consisting of panels constructed in a variety of different finishes.
- **Woodstain** A natural-wood finish that colours and protects a bare wooden surface.
- **Zigzag stitch** In sewing, a machine stitch that takes the form of a zigzag sawtooth and is used for neatening edges.

INDEX

ACKNOWLEDGMENTS

AUTHORS' ACKNOWLEDGMENTS

Many thanks to all those individuals who helped us to produce this book. However, the top of this list is firmly occupied by Jude, Sarah, and Helen. Thank you for your total professionalism and unerring ability to humour us and deal with all manner of innuendo over the past year.

PUBLISHER'S ACKNOWLEDGMENTS

Dorling Kindersley would like to thank the following:

Prop loan and provision of samples B & Q Plc (tools and materials); Biswell & Leggate (floor coverings); A.W. Champion (timber); Lead and Light (etching fluid); Leyland SDM (tools and materials); Metal Paint Ltd. (specialist paints); John Oliver (wall coverings).

Editorial and design assistance
Catherine Rubinstein and Penelope Cream for editorial assistance; Chris Bernstein for the index; Josephine Bryan for proofreading; Rachel Symons for design assistance; Mollie Gillard for picture research; and Dr Sue Davidson for checking health and safety guidelines.

Artworks Kuo Kang Chen and Halli Marie Verrinder.

Photographers Steve Tanner, Andy Crawford, and Sarah Ashun.
Photographic assistants Mary Wadsworth and Lee Walsh.

Hand models Toby Heran, Pepukai Makoni, Charmen Menzies, and Mary Wadsworth.

PICTURE CREDITS

Dorling Kindersley would like to thank the following for permission to reproduce their photographs:

Key: a above, b **below**, c **centre**, f **far**, l **left**, r **right**, t **top**.

Fired Earth: 59bc, 66c, 66cr, 97tr; **Jake Fitzjohns**: 14br; **Chris Forsey**: 17l; **Anna French Ltd.**: 53cr; **Robert Harding Syndication**: Dominic Blackmore/Homes & Ideas © IPC Magazines: 19clb, 19br, Homes & Gardens © IPC Magazines 42c; **Homestyle and Fads** (paint and wall coverings): 7tr, 9cl, 11bl, 11cla, 11cra, 12ca, 12cr, 15bl, 53c, 107tl, 107br, 107bl, 115bc, 121c; 121cla, 131br; **Marks & Spencer**: 112cfl; **Gwenan Murphy**: 15cr, 54bl; **Colin Poole**: 13bl, 118bc, 118br, /J. Brown 37bc, /M. Reeve 37br; **Sanderson**: 12bl, 13br; **Sunway** (Venetian blind collection): 112 cfr; Steve Tanner (for Perfect Home DMG Home Interest Magazines Ltd.). 12bc, **Steve Tanner/Perfect Home DMG Home Interest Magazines Ltd.**: 107tl; **Elizabeth Whiting & Associates**: 20cl, 59br, 112cl, 112cr; Andreas von Einsiedel 42cr, /Eric Karson 14bl; Brian Harrison 20bl; Michael Dunn 20br, 21tr, 65br; Peter Wolosynski 21bl; Tom Leighton 21tl, 125br.